Thomas Moore

Travels of an Irish Gentleman in Search of a Religion

Vol I

Thomas Moore

Travels of an Irish Gentleman in Search of a Religion
Vol I

ISBN/EAN: 9783744728379

Printed in Europe, USA, Canada, Australia, Japan

Cover: Foto ©Lupo / pixelio.de

More available books at **www.hansebooks.com**

TRAVELS

OF AN

IRISH GENTLEMAN

IN

SEARCH OF A RELIGION.

WITH

Notes and Illustrations

BY THE

EDITOR OF "CAPTAIN ROCK'S MEMOIRS."

IN TWO VOLUMES.

VOL. I.

LONDON:
PRINTED FOR
LONGMAN, REES, ORME, BROWN, GREEN, & LONGMAN,
PATERNOSTER-ROW.

1833.

CONTENTS

OF

VOL. I.

CHAPTER I.

Soliloquy up two pair of stairs.—Motives for embracing Protestantism.—Providential accident.—Anti-popery Catechism.—Broadside of Epithets.—Final resolution
  Page 1

CHAPTER II.

Sir Godfrey Kneller and St. Peter—Varieties of Protestantism.—Resolved to choose the best.—Adieu to Popish abominations 8

CHAPTER III.

Begin with the First Century.—Pope St. Clement.—St. Ignatius.—Real Presence.—Heresy of the Docetæ.—Tradition.—Relics of Saints . . . 13

CHAPTER IV.

Visions of Hermas.—Weekly Fasting.—Good Works.—Rector of Ballymudragget.—Rector no Faster.—Comparison between the Rector and Hermas . 22

CHAPTER V.

Second Century.—St. Justin the Martyr.—Transubstantiation.—St. Irenæus.—Papal Supremacy.—Sacrifice of the Mass.—Unwritten Tradition.—Old Man of the Sea . . . . . Page 28

CHAPTER VI.

Making the sign of the Cross.—Tertullian.—Veneration of Images.—Prayers for the Dead.—Determination to find Protestantism somewhere . . . 40

CHAPTER VII.

Great dearth of Protestantism.—Try Third and Fourth Centuries.—St. Cyprian.—Origen.—Primacy of St. Peter and the Pope.—St. Jerome.—List of Popish abominations 46

CHAPTER VIII.

Invocation of the Virgin.—Gospel of the Infancy, &c.—Louis XI.—Bonaventura.—St. Ambrose, St. Basil, and Doctor Doyle 65

CHAPTER IX.

Prayers for the Dead.—Purgatory.—Penitential discipline. Confession.—Origen.—St. Ambrose.—Apostrophe to the Shade of Father O'H * * . . . 72

CHAPTER X.

The Eucharist.—A glimpse of Protestantism.—Type, Figure, Sign, &c.—Glimpse lost again.—St. Cyril of Jerusalem.—St. Cyprian.—St. Jerom.—St Chrysostom.—Tertullian 81

CHAPTER XI.

Discipline of the Secret.—Concealment of the Doctrine of the Real Presence.—St. Paul.—St. Clement of Alexandria.—Apostolical Constitutions.—System of secresy, when most observed . . Page 91

CHAPTER XII.

Doctrine of the Trinity.—St. Justin.—Irenæus.—Apparent heterodoxy of the Fathers of the Third Century.—Accounted for by the Discipline of the Secret.—Tertullian, Origen, Lactantius, &c. . . 99

CHAPTER XIII.

Doctrine of the Incarnation.—Importance attached to it by Christ himself.—John, vi.—Ignatius.—Connexion between the Incarnation and the Real Presence.—Concealment of the latter doctrine by the Fathers.—Proofs of this concealment 113

CHAPTER XIV.

Concealment of the Doctrine of the Eucharist.—Proofs.—Calumnies on the Christians.—Protestant view of this Sacrament—*not* that taken by the early Christians 124

CHAPTER XV.

Concealment of the Eucharist—most strict in Third Century.—St. Cyprian—his timidity—favourite Saint of the Protestants.—Alleged proofs against Transubstantiation.—Theodoret.—Gelasius.—Believers in the Catholic Doctrine of the Eucharist, Erasmus, Pascal, Sir Thomas More, Fenelon, Leibnitz, &c. . 133

CHAPTER XVI.

Relaxation of the Discipline of the Secret, on the subject of the Trinity.—Doctrine of the Real Presence still concealed.—The Eucharists of the Heretics.—The Artotnrites, Hydroparastatæ, &c.—St. Augustin a strict observer of the Secret.—Similar fate of Transubstantiation and the Trinity . . . Page 147

CHAPTER XVII.

Fathers of the Fourth Century.—Proofs of their doctrine respecting the Eucharist.—Ancient Liturgies . 159

CHAPTER XVIII.

Visit to T———d-street Chapel.—Antiquity of the observances of the Mass.—Lights, Incense, Holy Water, &c.—Craw-thumpers.—St. Augustin a Craw-thumper. —Imitations of Paganism in the early Church . 177

CHAPTER XIX.

Ruminations.—Unity of the Catholic Church.—History of St. Peter's Chair.—Means of preserving Unity.— Irenæus.—Hilary.—Indefectibility of the one Church
188

CHAPTER XX.

A Dream.—Scene, a Catholic Church—time, the third century.—Angel of Hermas.—High Mass.—Scene shifts to Ballymudragget.—Rector's Sermon.—Amen Chorus 197

CHAPTER XXI.

Search after Protestantism suspended.—Despair of finding it among the Orthodox.—Resolve to try the Heretics.—Dead Sea of Learning.—Balance of Agreeableness between Fathers and Heretics . . Page 209

CHAPTER XXII.

The Capharnaites the first Protestants.—Discourse of our Saviour at Capernaum—its true import.—Confirmatory of the Catholic doctrine of the Eucharist 216

CHAPTER XXIII.

The Docetæ, the earliest heretics.—Denial of the Real Presence.—Simon Magus and his Mistress.—Simon a Protestant.—Delight at the discovery.—The Ebionites.—The Elcesaites 226

CHAPTER XXIV.

Scriptural learning of the Gnostics—their theories.—Account of the system of the Valentinians.—Celestial Family.—Sophia—her daughter.—Birth of the Demiurge.—Bardesanes 236

CHAPTER XXV.

The Gnostics, believers in Two Gods.—The Creator and the Unknown Father.—Their charges against the Jehovah of the Jews.—Marcion—his Antitheses.—Apelles.—Belief in Two Saviours.—Hatred of the Jewish Code.—Ophites.—Marriage of Jesus with Sophia Achamoth 246

CHAPTER XXVI.

Catalogue of Heresies.—The Marcosians, Melchisedecians, Montanists, &c.—Why noticed.—Clemens Alexandrinus inclined to Gnosticism.—Tertullian, a Montanist.—St. Augustin, a Manichæan . Page 260

CHAPTER XXVII.

Discovery, at last, of Protestantism among the Gnostics.—Simon Magus the author of Calvinism.—Calvinistic doctrines held by the Valentinians, Basilidians, Manichæans, &c. 269

CHAPTER XXVIII.

Another search for Protestantism among the orthodox as unsuccessful as the former.—Fathers the very reverse of Calvinists.—Proofs.—St. Ignatius, St. Justin, &c.—Acknowledged by Protestants themselves . 278

CHAPTER XXIX.

Return to Heretics.—Find Protestantism in abundance.—Novatians, Agnoetæ, Donatists, &c.—Aerius, the first Presbyterian.—Accusations of Idolatry against the Catholics.—Brought forward by the Pagans, as now by the Protestants.—Conclusion of the Volume . 287

NOTES 301

TRAVELS

OF

AN IRISH GENTLEMAN

IN

SEARCH OF A RELIGION.

CHAPTER I.

Soliloquy up two pair of stairs.—Motives for embracing Protestantism.—Providential accident.—Anti-popery Catechism.—Broadside of Epithets.—Final resolution.

It was on the evening of the 16th day of April, 1829,—the very day on which the memorable news reached Dublin of the Royal Assent having been given to the Catholic Relief Bill,—that, as I was sitting alone in my chambers, up two pair of stairs, Trinity College, being myself one of the everlasting "Seven Millions" thus liberated, I started suddenly, after a few moments' reverie, from my chair, and taking a stride across the room, as if to make trial of a pair of emancipated legs, exclaimed, "Thank God! I may now, if I like, turn Protestant."

The reader will see, at once, in this short speech, the entire course of my thoughts at that moment of exultation. I found myself free, not only from the penalties attached to being a Catholic, but from the point of honour which had till then debarred me from being any thing else. Not that I had, indeed, ever much paused to consider in what the faith I professed differed from others. I was as yet young,—but just entered into my twenty-first year. The relations of my creed with this world had been of too stirring a nature to leave me much thought to bestow on its concernments with the next; nor was I yet so much of the degenerate Greek in my tastes as to sit discussing what was the precise colour of the light of Mount Thabor when that "light of life," liberty, was itself to be struggled for.

I had, therefore, little other notion of

Protestants than as a set of gentlemanlike heretics, somewhat scanty in creed, but in all things else rich and prosperous, and governing Ireland, according to their will and pleasure, by right of some certain Thirty-nine Articles, of which I had not yet clearly ascertained whether they were Articles of War or of Religion.

The Roman Catholics, on the other hand, though myself one of them, I could not help regarding as a race of obsolete and obstinate religionists, robbed of every thing but (what was, perhaps, least worth preserving) their Creed, and justifying the charge brought against them of being unfit for freedom, by having so long and so unresistingly submitted to be slaves. In short, I felt—as many other high-spirited young Papists must have felt before me—that I had been not only enslaved, but degraded by belonging to such a race; and though, had adversity still frowned on our faith, I would have clung to it to the last, and died fighting for Transubstantiation and the Pope with the best, I was not sorry to be saved the doubtful glory of such martyrdom; and much as I rejoiced at the release of my fellow-sufferers from thraldom, rejoiced still more at the prospect of my own release from *them*.

While such was the state of my feelings with respect to the *political* bearings of my creed, I saw no reason, on regarding it in a religious point of view, to feel much more satisfied with it. The dark pictures I had seen so invariably drawn, in Protestant pamphlets and sermons, of the religious tenets of Popery, had sunk mortifyingly into my mind; and when I heard eminent, learned, and, in the repute of the world, estimable men representing the faith which I had had the misfortune to inherit as a system of damnable idolatry, whose doctrines had not merely the tendency, but the prepense design, to encourage imposture, perjury, assassination, and all other monstrous crimes, I was already prepared, by the opinions which I had myself formed of my brother Papists, to be but too willing a recipient of such accusations against them from others. Though, as man and as citizen, I rose indignantly against these charges, yet, as Catholic, I quailed inwardly under the fear that they were but too true.

In this state of mind it was that I had long looked forward to the great measure of Emancipation, both as the closing of that old, bitter, and hereditary contest in which the spiritual part of the question had been made subordinate to the temporal, and, more particularly, as a release for myself from that scrupulous point of honour which had hitherto kept me wedded, "for better, for worse," to Popery.

The reader has now been put in full possession of the meaning of that abrupt exclamation which, as I have said, burst from me on the evening of the 16th of April, in my room up two pair of stairs, Trinity College,—" Thank God! I may now, if I like, turn Protestant." No sooner had this pithy sentence broke from my lips than I resumed my seat and plunged again into reverie. The college clock was, I recollect, striking eight, at the time this absorption of my thinking faculties commenced, and the same orthodox clock had tolled the tenth hour before the question "Shall I, or shall I not, turn Protestant?" was in any fair train for decision. Even then, it was owing very much to an accident, which some good people would call providential, that Popery did not—for that evening, at least—maintain her ground. On the shelf of the book-case near me lay a few stray pamphlets, towards which, in the midst of my meditations, I, almost unconsciously, put forth my hand, and taking the first that presented itself, found that I had got hold of a small tract, in the form of a Catechism, against Popery, published near a century ago, and called "A Protestant's Resolution, showing his Reasons why he will not be a Papist, &c. &c." On opening the leaves of this tract, the first sentences that met my eyes were as follows:—

"Q.—What was there in the Romish Religion that occasioned Protestants to separate themselves from it?

"A.—In that it was a superstitious, idolatrous, damnable, bloody, traitorous, blind, blasphemous religion."

This broadside of epithets at once settled

the whole matter. What gentleman, indeed, thought I, could abide to remain longer in a faith to which, with any show of justice, such hard and indigestible terms could be applied? Accordingly, up sprung I, for the second time, from my now *un*easy chair, and brandishing aloft my clenched hand, as if in defiance of the Abomination of the Seven Hills, exclaimed, as I again paced about my chamber,—with something of the Ascendancy strut already perceptible,—" I *will* be a Protestant."

CHAPTER II.

Sir Godfrey Kneller and St. Peter.—Varieties of Protestantism.—Resolved to choose the best.—Adieu to Popish abominations.

I WAS now pretty much in the situation of Sir Godfrey Kneller, in the strange dream attributed to him, when having arrived, as he thought, at the entrance of Heaven, he found St. Peter there, in his capacity of gate-keeper, inquiring the name and religion of the different candidates for admission that presented themselves, and, still as each gave his answer, directing them to the seats allotted to their respective creeds. "And pray, sir," said the Saint, addressing Sir Godfrey in his turn, " what religion may you be of?"—" Why, truly, sir," said Sir Godfrey, " I am of no religion."—" Oh, then, sir," replied St. Peter, " you will be so good as to go in and take your seat where you please."

In much the same independent state of creed did I find myself at this crisis,—having before me the whole variegated field of Protestantism, with power to choose on what part of its wide surface I should settle. But though thus free, and with " a charter like the wind, to blow where'er I pleased,"—my position, on the whole, was hardly what could be called comfortable. It was like that of a transmigrating spirit in the critical interval between its leaving one body and taking possession of another; or rather like a certain ill-translated work, of which some wit has remarked that it had been taken *out* of one language without being put *into* any other.

Though as ignorant, at that time of my life, on all matters of religion, as any young gentleman brought up at a University—even when meant for holy orders—could well be, I had, by nature, very strong devotional feelings, and from childhood had knelt nightly to my prayers with a degree of trust in God's mercy and grace at which a professor of the Five Points would have been not a little scandalized. It was, therefore, with perfect conscientiousness and sincerity that I now addressed myself to the task of choosing a new religion ; and having made up my mind that Protestantism was to be the creed of my choice, resolved also that it should be Protestantism of the best and most approved description.

But how was this to be managed? In a sermon which I once heard preached by a Fellow of our University, there was an observation put strongly by the preacher which I now called to mind for my guidance in the inquiry I was about to institute. " In like manner (said the preacher) as streams are always clearest near their source, so the first ages of Christianity will be found to have been the purest." Taking this obvious position for granted, the deduction was of course evident that to the doctrines and practice of the early ages of the Church I must have recourse to find the true doctrines and practice of Protestantism ;—the changes which afterwards took place, as well in the tenets as the observances of Christians, having been, as the preacher told us, the cause of " that corrupt system of religion which has been entailed on the world under the odious name of Popery." To ascend, therefore, at once to that Aurora of our faith, and imbue myself thoroughly with the opinions and doctrines of those upon whom its light first shone, was, I could not doubt, the sole effectual mode of attaining the great object I had in view,—that of making myself a Protestant according to the purest and most orthodox pattern.

To the classical branch of the course taught in our University I had devoted a good deal of attention. My acquaintance, therefore, with Latin and Greek was sufficiently familiar to embolden me to enter on the study of the Fathers in their own languages; while, besides the access which I was allowed, as graduate, to the library of our College, I had also, through another channel, all the best editions of those holy writers placed at my command. Of the Scriptures my knowledge had hitherto been scanty; but the plan I now adopted was to make my study of the sacred volume concurrent with this inquiry into the writings of its first expounders; so that the text and the comment might, by such juxta-position, shed light on each other.

Behold me, then, with a zeal whose sincerity at least deserved some success, sitting down, dictionary in hand, to my task of self-conversion; having secured one great step towards the adoption of a new creed in the feeling little short of contempt with which I looked back upon the old one. Bidding a glad and, as I trusted, eternal adieu to the long catalogue of Popish abominations, to wit, Transubstantiation, Relics, Fasting, Purgatory, Invocation of Saints, &c. &c.—I opened my mind, a willing initiate, to those enlightening truths which were now, from a purer quarter of the heavens, to dawn upon me.

CHAPTER III.

Begin with the First Century.—Pope St. Clement.—St. Ignatius.—Real Presence.—Heresy of the Docetæ.—Tradition.—Relics of Saints.

THERE is, among those who consider the Catholic Church to have, in the course of time, fallen from its first purity, a considerable difference of opinion as to the period at which this apostasy commenced; some writers having been disposed to extend the golden period of the Church to as late a period as the seventh or eighth century*, while by others her virgin

---

* One of those who allow the "beaux jours de l'Église" (as he calls them) to have extended so far was the celebrated Huguenot minister, Claude,—celebrated, among other things, for the signal defeat which he sustained from the learned authors of the Perpétuité de la Foi. Of this great champion of Protestantism, so lauded in his day, it is curious to see what was the private opinion entertained by one who lived in his society, and is known not to have been unfriendly to his sect or its cause:— "Cet homme-là (says Longuerue) étoit bon à gouverner chez Madame la Maréchale de Schomberg, où il regnoit

era is confined within far less liberal limits*. My great object, however, being, as much as possible, "*integros accedere fontes*," I saw that the higher up, near the very source, I began my researches, the better; and, accordingly, with the writings of those five holy men who are distinguished by the title of Apostolical Fathers, as having all of them conversed with the Apostles or their disciples, I now commenced my studies.

Great, then, was my surprise,—not unaccompanied, I own, by a slight twinge of remorse,—when, in the person of one of these simple, apostolical writers, I found that I had popped upon a Pope—an actual Pope!—being the third Bishop, after St. Peter, of that very Church of Rome which I was now about to desert for her modern rival. This

---

souverainement; mais il n'étoit point savant. Parlez-moi, pour le savoir, d'Aubertin, de Daillé, de Blondel."

According to the Book of Homilies, "the Christian Religion was, unto the time of Constantine (A. D. 324), most pure and indeed golden."

* Priestley, for instance, to suit his purpose, considers the period till the death of Adrian (A. D. 138) as comprising the pure and virgin age of the Church.

primitive occupant of the See of Rome was St. Clement, one of those fellow-labourers of St. Paul, whose "names are written in the Book of Life;" and it was by St. Peter himself, as Tertullian tells us, that he had been ordained to be his successor. This proof of the antiquity and apostolical source of the Papal authority startled me not a little. "A Pope! and ordained by St. Peter!" exclaimed I, as I commenced reading the volume: "now, ' by St. Peter's Church, and Peter too,' this much surpriseth me." There was, however, still enough of the Papist lingering in my heart to make me turn over the pages of Pope St. Clement with peculiar respect; and I could not but see that, even in those simple, unpolemic times, when the actual exercise of authority could be so little called for, the jurisdiction of the See of Peter was fully acknowledged.

A schism, or, as St. Clement himself describes it, "a foul and unholy sedition*," having broken out in the Church of Corinth,

---

* Μιαράν και ανοσιον στασιν.

an appeal was made to the Church of Rome for its interference and advice, and the Epistle which this Holy Father addressed to the Corinthians in answer, is confessedly one of the most interesting monuments of Ecclesiastical Literature that have descended to us.

The next of these primitive followers of the Apostles whose writings engaged my attention was St. Ignatius, the immediate successor of the Apostle Peter in the See of Antioch. This holy man was by his contemporaries called Theophorus, or the God-borne, from a general notion that he was the child mentioned by Matthew and Mark, as having been taken up by our Saviour in his arms, and set in the midst of his disciples. It was, therefore, with a feeling of reverent curiosity that I approached his volume; and much as I had been, in my ignorance, astonished, to find a Pope, or Bishop of Rome, presiding* at such a period over the whole Christian

---

* The Epistle of St. Ignatius to the Romans, which was written in the first century, is addressed " to the Church that *presides* ($προκαθηται$) in the country of the Romans."

world, I was now infinitely more astounded and puzzled by what met my eyes in the pages of Ignatius, a writer nursed, as it were, in the very cradle of our faith, and who, as one of the first that followed in the footsteps of the Divine Guide, was among the last from whom I could have expected a doctrine so essentially Popish,—the invention, as I had always been led to suppose, of the darkest ages, and maintained in mockery, as well of reason, as of the senses,—the doctrine, in short, of a real, corporal Presence in the Eucharist!

In speaking of the Docetæ, or Phantasticks, a sect of hereticks who held that Christ was but, in *appearance*, Man,—a mere semblance or phantasm of humanity,—Ignatius says, " They stay away from the Eucharist and from prayer, *because they will not acknowledge the Eucharist to be the flesh of our Saviour Jesus Christ, that flesh which suffered for our sins.*" Now, when it is considered that the leading doctrine of the Docetæ was that the body assumed by

Christ was but *apparent*, there cannot be a doubt that the particular opinion of the orthodox to which they opposed themselves was that which held the presence of Christ's body in the Eucharist to be *real*. It is evident that a *figurative* or unsubstantial presence, such as Protestants maintain, would in no degree have offended their anti-corporeal notions; but, on the contrary, indeed, would have fallen in with that wholly spiritual view of Christ's nature which had led these heretics to deny the possibility of his incarnation.

This perplexing and irresistible proof, on the very threshold of my inquiry, of the existence of such a belief among the orthodox of the first century, threw me, I own, into a state of unspeakable amazement. I looked at the words again—rubbed my eyes, and again consulted my lexicon. But I had made no mistake;—there it was, in black and white, stark staring Popery. I had found language of a similar import, respecting the Eucharist, in other passages of the same Father;—in the Epistle to the Philadelphians, and in that also to the Romans. But had there existed only these notices, his precise opinion upon the subject might have been doubtful; and, as in many other cases, where the Fathers have happened to express themselves allegorically or obscurely, would have remained matter of controversy. But taken, as I have already said, with reference to the Docetæ, and representing the belief of those heretics, respecting the Eucharist, as wholly irreconcilable with the creed of the orthodox*, this passage in the Epistle to the Smyrnæans

---

* " It seems highly probable that Communicants, in St. Ignatius's days, were obliged expressly to acknowledge the Eucharist to be Christ's body and blood, by answering ' Amen' at the delivery of the Sacramental body and blood, as well as by joining in prayer to God that he would make them so; and because the Docetæ could not do this, therefore they absented themselves from the Christian Assemblies."—*Johnson.*

That this express acknowledgment of the Real Presence was required of communicants, in the first ages of the Church, appears from all the ancient Liturgies, and we have St. Augustin's authority that such was the meaning attached to the " Amen," in his times :—" Habet magnum vocem Christi sanguis in terra cum, eo accepto, ab omnibus gentibus respondetur Amen."—*Contra Faust.*

can admit of but one conclusion, namely, that the orthodox Christians of that day saw in the consecrated bread and wine, not any mere memorial, representation, type, or emblem,—not any such figurative substitute for the body of our Lord,—but his own real substance, corporally present and orally manducated.

To find myself thus back again in the very depths of Popery, after having so fondly fancied that I had emerged from them for ever, was, it must be owned, not a little trying to a neophyte's zeal;—nor had I well recovered from my surprise and perplexity at this sample of Popish *doctrine*, when, on turning to an account of the martyrdom of this same Father, I fell upon a no less glaring specimen of Popish *practice*. Ignatius, as is well known to all readers of martyrology, was delivered up to be devoured by lions in the amphitheatre at Rome. After the victim had been despatched, the faithful deacons who had accompanied him on his journey gathered up, as we are told, the few bones which the wild beasts had spared, and carrying them back to Antioch deposited them there religiously in a shrine, round which annually, on the day of his martyrdom, the Faithful assembled, and, in memory of his self-devotion, kept vigil around his relics!

It should have been mentioned, also,—to make the matter still worse,—that, when on his way through Asia to the scene of his sufferings, this illustrious Father, in exhorting the Churches to be on their guard against Heresy, impressed earnestly upon them " *to hold fast by the Traditions of the Apostles ;*"—thus sanctioning that twofold Rule of Faith, the Unwritten as well as the Written Word, which by all good Protestants is repudiated as one of the falsest of the false doctrines of Popery!

Marvellous to me, most marvellous, were these discoveries;—a Pope, Relics of Saints, Apostolical Traditions, and a Corporal Eucharist, all in the First Age of the Church! —who *could* have thought it?

CHAPTER IV.

Visions of Hermas.—Weekly Fasting.—Good Works.—Rector of Ballymudragget.—Rector no Faster.—Comparison between the Rector and Hermas.

AFTER turning over the two Epistles that remain of St. Barnabas and St. Polycarp, and learning but little, towards the object of my search, from either, it was with some pleasure I opened the pages of the pious and fanciful Hermas, and among his Visions, which breathe all the simplicity of an apostolic age, forgot myself, for some hours, as in a fairy tale. His recollections of his early love—his seeing the heavens open, as he knelt one day praying in a meadow, and beholding the maid whom he had loved looking out of the clouds to salute him, saying "Good day, Hermas!"—his account of the various visions in which "the Church of God" had appeared to him; now, in the shape of an aged matron, reading;—now, as a young maiden, clad all in white, and having a mitre on her head, over which the long hair fell shining;—through all these innocent and (as they were thought at the time) *inspired* fancies* I wandered with the good Father, in a sort of drowsy reverie, even as though I were myself the dreamer of his visions.

It was not till, in the course of my reading, I came to that part of his work called Precepts and Similitudes,—which were, as he says, revealed to him by his guardian angel, in the shape of a Shepherd,—that I was awakened to a recollection of the immediate object of my studies, and awakened, also, alas, to find myself once more in Popish company. This Father, be it recollected, was one of those distinguished Christians to whom St.

---

* Origen quotes the Shepherd as a work divinely inspired; and Ruffinus expressly styles it a "Book of the New Testament."—*Expos. in Symb. Apostol.* Whiston, too, with his usual ready belief in all that suits his purpose, considers the Shepherd to be a distinct inspired Book of itself, which "comes directly from our Saviour as the Apocalypse does."

Paul sends salutations in the Epistle to the Romans, and among the moral precepts which in this work he represents his angel to have communicated to him is the following:— "The first thing we have to do is to observe the commandments of God. If afterwards a man wishes to add thereunto any *good work*, such as *fasting*, he will receive the greater recompense."

Here again was sheer Popery, both in doctrine and practice—Satisfaction to God by Good Works, and one of those Good Works, Fasting!

To this latter observance, I had from my childhood entertained a peculiar aversion; and it was therefore with pain, as well as wonder, I now made the discovery that, in rigour of fasting, the early Christians outwent even our strictest Romanists. The Fast preparatory to Easter Day, which was one of total abstinence, was by some pious persons continued for the space of forty successive hours; and those who laugh at Papists now for fasting twice a week would have had equal grounds for laughing at the Primitive Christians, who, by the Apostolic Canons, were enjoined to a similar practice;—the only difference being that the appointed days of fasting, which were then Wednesday and Friday, are now Friday and Saturday*. Just before Easter, indeed, these latter days were also observed, as fast-days, and for this reason, that " in those days the bridegroom was taken away†." And this was the age to which I had been sent for emancipation from Popery!

These ancient Christians, too, contrived to

---

* The learned Bishop Beveridge, who supposes these Canons to have been framed by the disciples of the Apostles about the end of the second century, considers the Fasts therein enjoined to have been of apostolical institution.—*Codex Canon. Ec. &c.* Mosheim, too, allows that "those who affirm that, in the time of the Apostles, or soon after, the fourth and sixth days of the week were observed as Fasts, are not, it must be acknowledged, destitute of specious arguments in favour of their opinion."

† " But the days will come when the bridegroom shall be taken from them, and then shall they fast."—*Matthew*, ix. 15. St. Jerom, who pronounces Lent to be an apostolic institution, attributes the same high origin to the Saturday's Fast.

make the Good Work of Fasting subservient to another practice, reputed also among Good Works, alms-giving; the same Apostolic Canons informing us that whatever had been saved by abstinence was always laid out in relieving the necessities of the poor*.

How vividly now, as I sat leaning my elbow on the pages of "the Shepherd," did I call to mind what my own feelings had been, more than once, at my poor father's table, when it has happened that our rich neighbour, the Rector of Ballymudragget, has invited himself to dine with us, on a Friday, or other fast-day; and while his Reverence has sat feasting on the flesh and fowl provided purposely for his regale, I have found myself forced to put up with that sorry fare which " *Hopdance* cried for in Poor Tom's belly—two white herrings†;" and still more mortifying, had to bear the smile of consequential pity with which the Rector looked round on

---

* Την περισσειαν της νηστειας πενησιν επιχορηγειν.—*Ap. Const.* Lib. 5.

† Shakspeare's Lear.

his superstitious fellow-diners,—blessing his stars, no doubt, that the glorious Reformation had put all these matters on so much more civilized and gentlemanlike a footing.

Little did I then, for my consolation, know that I was borne out by the Apostolic Canons in my starvation; and when I now pondered over these things, and compared my fat friend, the Rector, with the simple Hermas, who can wonder if a slight doubt came over my mind, whether,—as far, at least, as a world to come is concerned,—it might not be safer to fast with the friend of St. Paul, than to feast with the Rector of Ballymudragget.

CHAPTER V.

Second Century.—St. Justin the Martyr.—Transubstantiation.—St. Irenæus.—Papal Supremacy.—Sacrifice of the Mass.—Unwritten Tradition.—Old Man of the Sea.

Thus far my progress in Protestantism had not been very rapid. I was determined, however, not to be lightly turned aside from my purpose; so, taking leave of the simple writers of the apostolic age, I launched boldly into the sacred literature of the Second Century, hoping to find, on my way, somewhat more of the Thirty-nine Articles, and somewhat less of Popery. I had but a short way, however, descended the stream, when I found my sails taken aback by the following passage in St. Justin the Martyr,—a man described by an ancient bishop as being near to the Apostles both in time and in virtue: " Nor do we take these gifts (in the Eucharist) as *common bread* and *common drink*; but as Jesus Christ, our Saviour, made man by the word of God, took flesh and blood for our salvation, so in the same manner we have been taught that the *food* which has been blessed by prayer, and by which our blood and flesh, *in the change*, are nourished, *is the flesh and blood of that Jesus incarnate.*"—Apol. 1.

The assertion of a real, corporal Presence by St. Ignatius had more than sufficiently startled me; but here was a still stronger case, a belief in the change of the elements, in actual Transubstantiation,—and this on the part of a Saint so illustrious as St. Justin! Verily, they who could send a Christian youth to learn Protestant doctrine of teachers like these, must plead guilty to the charge either of grossly deceiving him or being ignorant themselves.

We have already seen that the Primacy of the Roman See was, in the only case that called for an appeal to it, acknowledged in the first age of the Church; and I now found, in the second age, the same claim practically and universally recognized, both in the acts of the

Church and in the writings of her chief pastors. How little could I have anticipated such a discovery!—the "Great Harlot," the "Mother of the fornications and abominations of the earth" (as so often I had heard our college preacher style the Papacy), standing, in the pure morning of Christianity, supreme and unrivalled!

Accustomed, indeed, as I had long been to consider the papal jurisdiction as a usurpation of the dark ages, the clear proofs I now saw of the chain of succession by which its title is carried up and fixed fast in that "Rock" on which the Church itself is built, convinced and confounded me; nor, though myself but an "embryon immature" of Protestantism, could I help sympathising most heartily with all that a full-fledged follower of that faith must feel, on reading the following strong attestation of the Papal Primacy in St. Irenæus,— a writer, be it recollected, so near to the apostolical times as to have had for his instructor in Christianity a disciple of St John the Evangelist:

"We can enumerate those bishops who

were appointed by the Apostles and their successors down to ourselves, none of whom taught or even knew the wild opinions of these men (heretics) . . . However, as it would be tedious to enumerate the whole list of successions, I shall confine myself to that of *Rome, the greatest and most ancient and most illustrious Church*, founded by the glorious Apostles Peter and Paul; receiving from them her doctrine which was announced to all men, and *which, through the succession of her bishops, is come down to us.* Thus we confound *all those who, through evil designs, or vainglory, or perverseness, teach what they ought not;* for, to this Church, *on account of its Superior Headship*, every other must have recourse, that is, the faithful of all countries; in which Church has been preserved the doctrine delivered by the Apostles."—*Adv. Hæres. Lib. 3.*

Of Irenæus it must be, in truth, acknowledged that, though so apostolically educated, and graced by Photius with the title of " the Divine Irenæus*, ' he would have made but a

---

* Του Θεσπεσιου Ειρηναιου.

faithless subscriber to the Thirty-nine Articles. For only hear how this Saint speaks of the Sacrifice of the Mass*,—that " blasphemous fable," as the Thirty-First of those Articles terms it:—" Likewise he declared the cup to be his blood, and taught the new Oblation of the New Testament, which oblation the Church receiving from the Apostles offers it to God over all the earth." Again:—" Therefore, the offering of the Church which the Lord directed to be made over all the world was deemed a pure sacrifice before God and received by Him†."

---

* Anciently called the Sacrifice of the New Testament, or Catholic Sacrifice (Θυσια καθολικη.—*Chrysostom. Serm. de Cruce et Latrone*), the word Mass not having been introduced till about the time of St. Ambrose.

† See also Justin. Dial. cum Tryphon.

" The Centuriators of Magdeburgh,—whose zeal and acuteness displayed in the Protestant cause are well known—have been constrained reluctantly to own that the existence of the Sacrifice of the New Law stands recorded in the early monuments of Christianity; and on the passage of St. Irenæus here referred to, they express their acknowledgment in terms of indignation."—*Coombes's Essence of Religious Controversy.*

Consistently with his belief of a Sacrifice in the Eucharist, this Father maintained also, with Justin and Ignatius, the Real Presence of Christ's body and blood in that Sacrament; pronouncing it a miracle such as could not be supposed to exist, without admitting the Divinity of Him who had instituted it. " How," he asks, " can these heretics (those who denied that Christ was the Son of God) prove that the bread over which the words of thanksgiving have been pronounced *is* the body of their Lord and the cup his blood, while they do not admit that he is the Son, that is, the Word of the Creator of the World?"

To the same heretics, who, from their views of the corruption of matter, could not reconcile to themselves the doctrine of a resurrection of the body, he makes use of an argument founded, in like manner, on his belief of the reality of Christ's Presence and the transubstantiation of the elements:—" When (says he) the mingled chalice and the broken bread receive the word of God, they *become* the

Eucharist of the body and blood of Christ*, by which the substance of our flesh is increased and strengthened. How then can they pretend, that this flesh is not susceptible of eternal life which is nourished by the body and blood of the Lord and is his member?"

On the subject of Unwritten Tradition,—that contested source of so much of the doctrine, practice, and power of Rome, this Father's testimony brings with it double weight, inasmuch as he not only asserts, in all his writings, the high authority of Tradition, but was himself one of the earliest and brightest links in that chain of oral delivery which has descended to the

---

* There is yet a stronger passage to this purpose in one of those Fragments attributed to Irenæus, which were published in 1715 by Dr. Pfaff, from manuscripts in the King of Sardinia's library;—where, in describing the ceremonies of the Sacrifice, it is said that the Holy Spirit is invoked that he may *make* the bread the body of Christ and the cup the blood of Christ. Much doubt, however, has been thrown upon the genuineness of these Fragments, both by Maffei, who objected to them on their first appearance, and by the remarks of the ever judicious Lardner afterwards.

Church of Rome from the apostolic age. Referring to his own master, Polycarp, who had been the disciple of St. John the Evangelist*, he says—" Polycarp always taught these things, which he had learned from the Apostles, which he delivered to the Church, and which alone are true." In a fragment of another of his writings there occurs a most impressive and interesting passage to the same effect. Addressing a heretic, named Florinus, who had adopted the errors of the Valentinians, he says—" Those opinions the Presbyters before us, who also conversed with the Apostles, have not delivered to you. For I saw you, when I was very young, in the Lower Asia with Polycarp. . . . I better remember the affairs of that time than those which have lately happened; the things which we learn in our childhood growing up with the soul and uniting themselves to it. Insomuch that

---

* By many also supposed to have been the Angel of the Church of Smyrna, to whom the Epistle in the second chapter of the Book of Revelation was directed to be sent.

I can tell the place in which the Blessed Polycarp sat and taught, and his going out and coming in; and the manner of his life and the form of his person; and the discourses he made to the people, and how he related his conversation with St. John, and others who had seen the Lord; and how he related their sayings, and what he had heard from them concerning the Lord; both concerning his miracles and his doctrine, as he had received them from the eye-witnesses of the Word of Life: all which Polycarp related agreeable to the Scriptures. These things I then, through the mercy of God toward me, diligently heard and attended to, recording them not on paper, but upon my heart; and, through the grace of God, I continually renew my remembrance of them."

Could we now summon to earth the shade of this holy Father,—this Saint, so "nourished up in the words of faith and of good doctrine,"—with what face can we imagine a Protestant, an upstart of the Reformation, to stand forth, in contradiction to so orthodox a spirit, and pronounce the Unwritten Word of the Catholic Church to be but an inheritance of imposture, the jurisdiction of the See of St. Peter a rank usurpation, and the Sacrifice of the Holy Mass " a blasphemous fable?"

If any thing more were wanting to show the deep sense which this Father entertained of the reverence due to the authority and traditions of the Church, we should find it in the few following passages from his writings:— "*In explaining the Scriptures, Christians are to attend to the Pastors of the Church*, who, by the ordinance of God, have received the inheritance of truth, with the succession of their Sees." " The tongues of nations vary, *but the virtue of tradition is one and the same every where;* nor do the churches in Germany believe or teach differently from those in Spain, Gaul, the East, Egypt or Lybia." " *Supposing the Apostles had not left us the Scriptures, ought we not still to have followed the ordinance of Tradition*, which they consigned to those to whom they committed the Churches? *It is this ordinance of Tradition which many nations of barbarians, believing in Christ, follow without the use of letters or ink."*—Adv. Hær. Lib. 4.

It will easily be believed that, at the close of this long day's studies, I felt utterly disheartened and wearied with my pursuit. I had now found sanctioned by the authority of the Church's earliest champions,—some of them men who " had the preaching of the Apostles still sounding in their ears,"—six no less Popish points of faith and observance than—1. The acknowledgment of a Sovereign Pontiff*; 2. A Reverence due to Relics; 3. Satisfaction to God by fasting, alms-deeds, &c.; 4. The authority of Tradition; 5. A Corporeal Presence in the Eucharist; and 6. The Sacrifice of the Mass. Who can wonder if, after all this, I despaired of ridding myself of Popery? Heaving a heavy sigh, as I closed my ponderous folios, and with a sort of oppressed sensation, as if the Pope were himself

---

* We find this very title of " Sovereign Pontiff" given to the Bishop of Rome by no less high and ancient an authority than Tertullian.

bodily on my back, I went to bed feeling much as Sinbad the sailor would have done, if, after having shaken off, as he thought, the troublesome little old Man of the Sea, he felt the legs of the creature again fastening round his neck.

CHAPTER VI.

Making the sign of the Cross.—Tertullian.—Veneration of Images.—Prayers for the Dead.—Determination to find Protestantism somewhere.

On the following morning I rose,—thanks to the recruiting power of sleep,—somewhat recovered from the rebuffs of the few preceding days, and feeling, on the whole, as well and *Protestant* as could be expected. At least, my horror of returning to Popery was as strong as ever; though my chances of becoming a good Protestant,—or, indeed, finding out what a good Protestant was,—had become all but desperate. I was, therefore, pretty much in the " unhoused condition" of that sect of heretics, called Basilidians, who described themselves as being no longer Jews, but still not yet Christians.

Of the disagreeable, but apostolic, practice of weekly fasting I have already spoken; but there was another Popish custom, against which, as a badge of anile superstition, I still more indignantly rebelled;—and this was the practice of making the sign of the Cross on the forehead, after grace, at meals. The feeling of shame with which, in my youth, I used to perform this overt act of Popery, in the presence of Protestants, I shall never forget*. Nor do I appear to have been, in this feeling, at all singular among my fellow Catholics, as I have observed that, ever since the two Religions have come to be on dining terms with each other, the practice has been almost wholly discontinued; insomuch that he must be a primitive Catholic indeed, who, in the present times, would venture to *bless himself* (as the operation is called) in good company.

"This, at least," said I to myself, pettishly,

---

* It appears from occasional rebukes, in the Fathers, on this subject, that a similar shame of being seen to make the sign of the cross was not unknown even among ancient Catholics.—" Let us not be ashamed (says St. Cyril) to confess Him who was crucified; let the σφραγις (the sign of the cross) be confidently made upon the forehead with the finger."

as I opened a huge volume of Tertullian,—"this monk's trick, at least, can assuredly never have received any sanction from the orthodox Christians of the early Church." The words had scarcely passed my lips, when, on turning to this Father's account of the modes and customs of his fellow Christians, I read, to my astoundment, as follows:—" We sign ourselves with the sign of the cross in the forehead, whenever we go from home or return, when we put on our clothes or our shoes, when we go to the bath, or sit down to meat, when we light our candles, when we lie down and when we sit." Here was crossing enough, God knows,—crossing enough, in a single day of Tertullian's, to serve the most particular old Catholic lady in all Ireland for a week.

There now remained little else to fill up the measure of what are called Popish superstitions but Veneration of Images and Prayers for the Dead;—and to both these I found the same eminent Father lending his sanction. In speaking of the wife who survives her husband, he desires that she should "pray for her husband's soul, solicit for him refreshment, and offer on the anniversaries of his death." In another place, too, we find him tracing this practice to apostolical traditions, not enforced, as he says, by the positive words of Scripture, but delivered down from his predecessors;—thus not only upholding the papistical usage of praying for the Dead, but deriving his authority for it through that equally papistical channel, Tradition!

With respect to Images, the use of which, as memorials, was derived also by the early Christians from tradition, a passing sentence of Tertullian, in which he mentions, as though it were of common occurrence, the pictures of Christ upon the communion-cups*, is a sufficient proof that the use of images had been,

---

* In a curious work on the Eucharistic Cups of the ancient Christians (by Doughty), the author has collected, with much industry, an account of the different materials of which these vessels were formed, from wood up to crystal, onyx, &c. and among the images upon them he particularly specifies that of the Crucified Saviour, and the good Shepherd carrying the lamb on his shoulders.

at the time he wrote, long prevalent. There appears little doubt, indeed, that Reformed eyes would have been shocked by such "idolatrous" representations, not only in the second century of Christianity, but most probably from its very earliest periods*. From the same fondness for religious memorials, we find St. Clement of Alexandria, in the same century, recommending to Christians to wear the figure of a fish engraved on their rings,—the fish being a symbol of the name of Christ †.

I had now, in addition to the six "plague-spots of Popery," which I had already, in this her virgin period, counted on the fair face of the Church, to number also the three following,—viz. 7. Prayers for the Dead.—8.

* In the year 814, when Leo, the Armenian, assembled several bishops in order to induce them to break images, Euthymius, metropolitan of Sardis, thus addressed him:—"Know, sire, that for 800 years and more since Christ came into the world, he has been painted and adored in his image. Who will be bold enough to abolish so ancient a tradition?"

† Clem. Alexand. Opera curà Potteri, p. 288.

Veneration of Images. And 9. Crossing, without end! Assuredly, any one less determined than myself to find Protestantism *somewhere*, would have given up the chase in despair. But I was still resolved to persevere. I had bid too solemn a farewell to Popery to allow of my revoking the step now with a good grace. Besides, it is but fair to confess,—what I ought perhaps to have confessed somewhat sooner,—that, in addition to a very conscientious desire of exchanging my religion for a better, I had also some motives of a more mundane and, I may add, tender nature, which had considerable weight in determining me to become a Protestant as soon as possible;—motives which, though of that class usually styled private and delicate, I shall, in some future chapter, venture to communicate to the reader.

CHAPTER VII.

Great dearth of Protestantism.—Try Third and Fourth Centuries.—St. Cyprian.—Origen.—Primacy of St. Peter and the Pope.—St. Jerome.—List of Popish abominations.

Though I had now pretty well convinced myself that if, as Protestants assure us, the pure original of their Creed is to be found in the first ages, it must be found there in some such modest and unobtrusive shape as that of a certain tragic author's " moon behind a cloud," I did not, even yet, allow myself to despair of catching, at least, a glimpse of this retired luminary. I therefore continued my Inquest and, summoning the Fathers of the two following centuries before me, resolved to try whether, by dint of close cross-questioning, I should be able to detect a single Protestant among them. But no; the answer of all was the same,—they belonged to the one Catholic

Church; to that Church, says St. Cyprian, " which, imbrued with the light of the Lord, sends forth her rays over the whole earth." When asked to name the centre from which this Catholic light radiates, the same Saint points to Rome, to the Chair of Peter, and " *the principal Church* (as he says emphatically) whence the Sacerdotal Unity took its rise."—*Ep.* 55.

Thus foiled, I flew to Origen, with somewhat, perhaps, of a hope that, being but a questionable Saint, he might prove a good Protestant. But my success was no better; I found him as eager for the Primacy of St. Peter and the Pope as his brethren, and, on the subject of exclusive salvation, as Catholic as need be : " Let no one," he says, " persuade, let no one deceive himself; out of this house, that is, *out of the Church, there is no salvation.*"—Hom. 3 in Josue. By St. Jerome this monopoly of heaven was, I saw, asserted with no less vigour :—" *I know that the Church is founded upon Peter,* that is, on a Rock. Whoever eateth the lamb out of that house, is a profane man. Whoever is not in the Ark shall perish by the flood."—*Ep.* 14 *ad Dam.* To a wight, like me, just tottering upon the edge of said Ark,—if not already off,—this metaphoric hint was comfortable!

On all those Popish points of belief and practice which, as I have shown, were sanctioned by the Fathers of the two First Centuries, I found the doctrine of those of the Third and Fourth precisely the same;— only put forth more copiously in detail, and enforced by richer stores of ingenuity and learning. To bring forward, indeed, all the testimonies that might, but too triumphantly, be cited to prove that, in those times, Christianity and Popery were convertible terms, would be to transcribe the greater part of the writings of the four first ages, from the simple Hermas down to the learned and rhetorical St. Chrysostom. I shall therefore content myself with adding to what I have already said of the Primitive times, a few specimens of the doctrine held by the leading Fathers of the third and fourth centuries, on some of the principal points at issue between the Church of Rome and her opponents.

AUTHORITY OF THE CHURCH.—TRADITION.

Tertullian.—" To know what the Apostles taught, that is, what Christ revealed to them, *recourse must be had to the Churches* which they founded, and which they instructed by word of mouth and by their Epistles."—*De Præscrip. c. 21.*

" Of these (certain practices in the administration of Baptism) and other usages, if you ask for the written authority of the Scriptures, none will be found. *They spring from Tradition, which practice has confirmed and obedience ratified.*"—De Corona Militis, c. 3, 4. " *To the Scriptures, therefore, an appeal must not be made* . . . . the question is, to whom was that doctrine committed by which we are made Christians? for where this doctrine and this faith shall be found, there

---

* This Father, having embraced Christianity about the year 185 and died in 216, is usually claimed as belonging alike to both Centuries.

will be the truth of the Scriptures and their expositions, and of all Christian Traditions."—*De Præscrip. c.* 19.

Origen.—"As there are many who think they believe what Christ taught, and some of these differ from others, it becomes necessary that all should profess that doctrine which came down from the Apostles, and now continues in the Church. *That alone is truth which in nothing differs from ecclesiastical and apostolical tradition.*"—Præf. lib. 1. de Princip. " As often as the heretics produce the Canonical Scriptures in which every Christian agrees and believes, they seem to say, Lo! with us is the word of truth. *But to them* (the heretics) *we cannot give credit, nor depart from the first and ecclesiastical tradition. We can believe only as the succeeding Churches of God have delivered.*"—Tract. 29 in Mat.

Lactantius.—" The Catholic Church alone retains the true worship. This is the source of truth, this is the dwelling of faith."—*Inst. l.* 4. *c.* 30.

Cyprian.—" It is easy to minds that are

religious and simple to lay aside error, and to discover truth: *for if we turn to the source of Divine Tradition, error ceases *."*—Ep. 63.

Eusebius.—" Which truths, *though they be consigned to the Sacred Writings, are still, in a fuller manner, confirmed by the Traditions of the Catholic Church,* which Church is diffused over all the earth. This *unwritten Tradition confirms and seals the testimonies of the Holy Scriptures."*—Dem. Evang. lib. 1.

Basil.—" Among the dogmas of the Church there are some contained in the Scriptures, and some come from Tradition; *but both have an equal efficacy in the promotion of piety."*— De Spirit. Sanct. c. 27. " *In my opinion, it is apostolical to adhere to unwritten Traditions."*—Ibid. c. 29. " *It is the common aim of all the enemies of sound doctrine, to shake the solidity of our faith in Christ by annulling*

---

* On this passage St. Augustin remarks:—" The advice which St. Cyprian gives to recur to the Tradition of the Apostles, and thence to bring down the series to our own times, is excellent, and manifestly to be followed." —De Bapt. contra Donatist. l. 5. c. 26.

apostolical Tradition . . . . they dismiss the unwritten testimony of the Fathers as a thing of no value."—Ib. c. 10.

Epiphanius.—"*We must look also to Tradition; for all things cannot be learned from the Scriptures.*"

Chrysostom.—"Hence it is manifest that they (the Apostles) did not deliver all things by means of Epistles, but that they made many communications without writing; and that both are equally entitled to credence. *It is a tradition, ask no further.*"—Hom. 4. in 2 Thess.*

PRIMACY OF THE SUCCESSORS OF ST. PETER.

Some of the strong testimonies, on this point, of St. Irenæus, St. Cyprian, &c. have already been laid before the reader.

Cyprian.—" Nevertheless that he (Christ) might clearly establish unity, he formed *one See*, and by his authority fixed the origin of

---

* On the passage of St. Paul:—" Therefore, brethren, stand fast, and hold the traditions which ye have been taught, whether by word, or our epistle."

this same unity by beginning from one. The other apostles were accordingly, like Peter, invested with an equal participation of honour and power; but the beginning is built on unity. *The Primacy is given to Peter that there might be exhibited one Church of Christ and one See.*"—De Unitat. Eccles.

Jerom.—(In a letter to Pope Damasus.) "I am following no other than Christ, united to the communion of your Holiness, that is, to the Chair of Peter. I know that the Church is founded upon that Rock."—*Ep.* 14. *ad Damasum.* "I cease not to proclaim, *He is mine who remains united to the Chair of Peter.*"

Chrysostom.—"For what reason did Christ shed his blood? Certainly, to gain those sheep *the care of which he committed to Peter and his successors.*"

SATISFACTION TO GOD BY PENITENTIAL WORKS.

Cyprian.—"The Lord must be invoked; must be appeased by our satisfaction."—De

Lapsis. " Before Him let the soul bow down: *to Him let our sorrow make satisfaction:* . . . . . By fasting, by tears, and by moaning, let us appease, as he himself admonishes, his indignation."—*Ib.* " *Purge away your sins by works of justice, and by alms-deeds which may save the soul.* God can pardon: he can turn away his judgment. He can pardon the penitent who implores forgiveness; he can accept for him the supplications of others; or should *he move him more by his own works of satisfaction, and thus disarm his anger,* the Lord will repair his strength, whereby he shall be invigorated anew*."—*Ib.*

* See Bossuet's defence of the language of St. Cyprian, on this subject, in answer to M. Jurien. " *Il faut, dit-il* (Saint Cyprien), *satisfaire à Dieu pour ses péchés;* mais il faut aussi *que la satisfaction soit reçue par notre Seigneur.* Il faut croire que tout ce qu'on fait n'a rien de parfait ni de suffisant en soi-même; puisqu'après tout, quoique nous fassions, nous ne sommes que de serviteurs inutiles et que nous m'avons pas même à nous glorifier du peu que nous faisons, puisque, comme nous l'avons déjà rapporte tout nous vient de Dieu par Jésus Christ, en qui seul nous avons accès auprès du Père."—*Avertissemens aux Protestans.* Such is the much misrepresented doctrine of Catholics on this point.

Ambrose.—" Let Christ see thee weeping, that he may say, ' Blessed are they that mourn, for they shall be comforted' (Mat. v. 4.). Therefore did he immediately pardon Peter, because he wept bitterly; and if thou weep in like manner, Christ will look on thee, and thy sin will be cancelled. . . . . . Let no consideration then withhold thee from *doing penance.* In this imitate the Saints, and let their tears be the measure of thy own."—*De Pœnit.* c. 10.

PRAYERS FOR THE DEAD.

Cyril of Jerusalem.—" Then (in the Sacrifice of the Mass) *we pray for the Holy Fathers and the Bishops that are dead; and, in short, for all those who are departed this life in our communion;* believing that the souls of those, for whom the prayers are offered,

The language of St. Augustin respecting this doctrine is fully as *Popish* as that of St. Cyprian :—" It is not enough," he says, " that the sinner change his ways, and depart from his evil works, unless by penitential sorrow, by humble tears, by the sacrifice of a contrite heart, and by alms-deeds, he *make satisfaction to God* for what he has committed."—*Homil.* l. T. x.

receive very great relief, while this holy and tremendous victim lies upon the altar."—*Catech. Mystag.* 5

Ambrose.—(In his Funeral Oration on the two Emperors, Valentinians). "Blessed shall you both be if my prayers can avail any thing. No day shall pass, in which I will not mention you with honour; no night in which you shall not partake of my prayers. In all my oblations I will remember you."

Epiphanius.—" *There is nothing more opportune, nothing more to be admired, than the rite which directs the names of the Dead to be mentioned.* They are aided by the Prayer which is offered for them, though it may not cancel all their faults.—We mention both the just and sinners, in order that for the latter we may obtain mercy."—*Hær.* 55.

Chrysostom.—" It is not in vain that oblations and prayers are offered and alms given for the dead. So has the Divine Spirit ordained that we might mutually assist one another."—*Homil.* 21. " *Not without reason was it ordained by the Apostle, that in cele-*

brating the Sacred Mysteries, the Dead should be remembered; for they well knew what advantage would thence be derived to them."—*Homil. 3. in Epist. ad Philip.**

INVOCATION OF SAINTS AND OF THE BLESSED VIRGIN.

Origen.—" We may be allowed to say of all the holy men who have quitted this life, retaining their charity towards those whom

---

* On the subject of Prayers for the Dead there occurs an interesting passage in St. Ephrem of Edessa, which appears to have escaped the notice of my friend. In a work entitled his Testament, this pious Father thus speaks:—" My brethren, come to me, and prepare me for my departure, for my strength is wholly gone. Go along with me in psalms and in your prayers, and please constantly to make oblations for me. When the thirtieth day shall be completed, then remember me; for the dead are helped by the offerings of the living.—Now listen with patience to what I shall mention from the Scriptures. Moses bestowed blessings on Reuben after the third generation (Deut. xxxiii. 6.); but, if the Dead are not aided, why was he blessed? Again, if they be insensible, hear what the Apostle says:—' If the dead rise not again at all, why are they then baptized for them?' (1 Cor. xv. 29.)"

they left behind, that they are anxious for their salvation, and that they assist them by their prayers and their mediation with God. For it is written in the books of the Maccabees, 'This is Jeremiah, the prophet of God, who always prays for the people.'—*Lib. 3. in Cant. Cantic.* ' I will fall down on my knees, and, *not presuming, on account of my crimes, to present my prayer to God, I will invoke all the saints to my assistance.* O ye saints of Heaven, I beseech you with a sorrow full of sighs and tears, fall at the feet of the Lord of Mercies for me, a miserable sinner.' "—*Lib. 2. de Job.*

Cyprian.—" Let us be mindful of one another in our prayers; with one mind, and with one heart, in this world, and in the next, let us always pray, with mutual charity relieving our sufferings and afflictions. And may the charity of him who, by the divine favour, shall first depart hence, still persevere before the Lord; may his prayer, for our brethren and sisters, be unceasing."—*De Habitu Virg.*

Athanasius.—" Hear now, oh daughter of

David; incline thine ear to our prayers.—We raise our cry to thee. *Remember us, oh! most Holy Virgin,* and for the feeble eulogiums we give thee, grant us great gifts from the treasures of thy graces, thou, who art full of grace.—Hail, Mary, full of grace, the Lord is with thee. *Queen and Mother of God, intercede for us.*"—Serm. in Annunt.

Hilary.—" According to Raphael, speaking to Tobias, there are Angels who serve before the face of God, and who convey to him the prayers of the suppliant.—It is not the character of the Deity that stands in need of this intercession, but our infirmity does.—God is not ignorant of any thing that we do; but the weakness of man, to supplicate and to obtain, calls for the ministry of the spiritual intercession."—*In Psalm.* 129.

Basil.—(In celebrating the Feast of the Forty Martyrs) " O ye common guardians of the human race, co-operators in our prayers, most powerful messengers, stars of the world and flowers of Churches, let us join our prayers with yours."—*Hom.* 19.

Ephrem of Edessa.—" I entreat you, oh! Holy Martyrs, who have suffered so much for the Lord, that you would intercede for us with Him that he bestow his grace on us."—*Encom. in SS. Mart.* " *We fly to thy patronage, Holy Mother of God;* protect and guard us, under the wings of thy mercy and kindness.—Most merciful God, *through the intercession of the most Blessed Virgin Mary, and of all the Angels, and of all the Saints,* show pity to thy creature."—*Serm. de Laud. B. Mar. Virg.*

RELICS AND IMAGES.

Hilary.—" The holy blood of the Martyrs is every where received, and their venerable bones daily bear witness."—*L. contra Constant.*

Basil.—" If any one suffer for the name of Christ, his remains are deemed precious: and, if any one touch the bones of a martyr, he becomes partaker, in some degree, of his holiness, on account of the grace residing in them. Wherefore, 'precious in the sight of God is the death of his Saints.'"—*Serm. in Psalm.* 115.

"I receive the Apostles, the Prophets and the Martyrs. I invoke them to pray for me, and that by their intercession God may be merciful to me and forgive my transgressions. For this reason I revere and honour their images, especially since we are taught to do so by the tradition of the holy Apostles; and so far from these being forbidden us, they appear in our Churches."—*Ep. ad Julian**.

Ephrem.—"The grace of the divine spirit, which works miracles in them, ever resides in the Relics of the Saints."—*In Encom. omnium Mart.*

Ambrose.—"I honour, therefore, in the body of the Martyr, the wounds that he re-

---

* In quoting this Epistle to Julian, as from the pen of St. Basil, my young friend has not shown his usual accuracy. The fragment from which the above passage is taken, though extant among the Acts of the Second Nicene Council, is given up, I believe, as spurious, by the most judicious Catholic writers; and even the zealous Baronius, though he produces the fragment, forbears cautiously from laying any stress upon it, as authority.

ceived in the name of Christ; I honour the memory of that virtue which shall never die; I honour those ashes which the confession of Faith has consecrated; I honour in them the seeds of eternity; I honour that body which has taught me to love the Lord, and not to fear death for his sake."—*Serm.* 55.

Chrysostom.—"Next to the power of speech, the monuments of Saints are best adapted, when we look on them, to excite us to the imitation of their virtues. Here when any one stands, he feels himself seized by a certain force; the view of the shrine strikes on his heart; he is affected, as if he that there lies were present, and offered up prayers for him. Thus does a certain alacrity come over him, and, changed almost to another man, he quits the place. For this reason, then, has God left us the Remains of the Saints."—*Lib. contra Gent.* "That which neither riches nor gold can effect, the Relics of Martyrs can. Gold never dispelled diseases nor warded off death; but the bones of Martyrs have done both. In the days of our forefathers, the former happened; the latter in our own."—*Homil. 67. de St. Drosid. Mart.*

Gregory of Nyssa.—(In his Oration on the Feast of the Martyr Theodorus) " When any one enters such a place as this, where the memory of this just man and his relics are preserved, his mind is first struck, while he views the structure and all its ornaments, with the general magnificence that breaks upon him. The artist has here shown his skill in the figures of animals and the airy sculpture of the stone, *while the painter's hand is most conspicuous in delineating the high achievements of the Martyr. . . . . . .*
. . . The figure of Christ is also beheld looking down upon the scene."

Nilus.—" In the chancel of the most sacred temple, towards the east let there be one and only one Cross . . . . *Let the sacred temple be filled with pictures well executed by the most celebrated artists, representing the most remarkable events of the Old and New Testaments;* that the unlettered and those who are incapable of reading the divine

Scriptures may, by the sight of the picture, be instructed in the virtuous deeds of those who have served the true God, according to his own will and command."—*Lib.* 4. *Ep.* 61.

CHAPTER VIII.

Invocation of the Virgin.—Gospel of the Infancy, &c.—Louis XI.—Bonaventura.—St. Ambrose, St. Basil, and Doctor Doyle.

In the foregoing list, containing a few of those "abominations" of Popery, which I found sanctioned by the highest authorities of the Christian Church, there is one placed under the head of "Invocation of Saints," to which I had not before adverted, namely, the devotion (or, as Protestants will have it,) idolatry paid by Papists to the Blessed Virgin. There appears no doubt that this worship, within the due bounds to which all rational Catholics would confine it, formed a part of the devotions of Christians, from the very first ages of the Church. In the Second Century we find Irenæus, the great light of that age, attributing such power to the intercession of the Virgin with God, as to suppose her the advocate, in heaven, for the fallen mother of mankind, Eve. The Gospel of the Infancy of Jesus, a work referred to the same period, and which, though manifestly an imposture*, may, at least, be depended upon, as an echo of the tone prevalent among the orthodox of its times, in relating the circumstances which took place previously to our Lord's nativity, gives to the Virgin simply the name of "Mary," but immediately after that event, styles her the "Divine Mary," and adds that Churches were, in those times, dedicated to her honour†.

---

* With this Gospel another apocryphal work, of the same high antiquity, is usually joined, to wit, the Gospel of the Birth of Mary, in which it is declared that the object of her espousals with Joseph was, not that he might make her his wife, but that he might be the guardian of her perpetual Virginity; the High Priest having said to him, "Thou art the person chosen to take the Virgin of the Lord, to keep her for him."

† The minister, Jurieu, contended that the claims of the Virgin to invocation or worship were not admitted till after that decision of the Council of Ephesus, which, in opposition to Nestorius, pronounced Mary to be the Mother of God. It is well answered, however, by Bossuet

In the irritation which, I own, I could not help feeling at the discovery of this fresh proof of Popery, in the early ages of the Church, I found myself secretly wishing that it might also be in my power to detect, in those times, the same extravagant follies respecting the worship of the Virgin, which, in after ages, brought such discredit upon the religion that was made responsible for them, and by which alone, indeed, most Protestants form their judgment of the Catholic faith on this subject*. I allude not so much to the gross extravagances of those who have installed the Virgin as a Fourth

---

that the very Church in which that Council was held bore testimony to the honours already paid to the Virgin by its having been dedicated to her name. He refers also to a circumstance which, long before the sitting of that Council, St. Gregory of Nazianzum had related of a female martyr in the third century, who prayed to the Blessed Mary "to aid a virgin who was in peril."

* The Lutheran Goetzius, assuming charitably that female saints,—Mary, Anne, Catherine, Margaret, &c. (as he enumerates them),—form the principal object of worship with the Catholics, calls their faith "a womanish Religion"—*religio muliebris.* See his Meletemata Annabergensia.

Person of the Godhead, or to such superstitious follies as that of Louis XI., who, by a formal contract, made over to the Mother of God all right and title in the fee and privileges of the Comte de Boulogne,—not so much to these blasphemous absurdities do I allude, as to that injudicious excess of zeal which led Bonaventura and other distinguished Catholics to claim for the Virgin a rank in the scale of superior beings much higher than either reason or true piety would assign to her*.

* The absurdity of the learned Lipsius (one of those many literati, whose whole due of fame is, as it were, discounted to them while living) in bequeathing his best fur cloak to the Virgin on his deathbed, drew down from the Netherland wits a burst of ridicule upon his memory which the defence of the bequest by his friend Wowerius (Assertio Lipsiani Donari) was but ill calculated to extinguish.

Of the lengths to which some pious enthusiasts in the cause of the Virgin have gone, many curious instances might be collected. For example, the following Thesis, put forth by the Récollets of Liege, in 1676.—" Frequens confessio et communio, et cultus B. Virginis, etiam in iis, qui gentiliter vivunt, sunt signum predestinationis;" and, still more absurd, the assertion of a Portuguese Jesuit, Francis Mendoza, " impossibile esse ut B. Virginis cultor in æternum damnetur." These are, to be sure, wretched

So far from finding, however, in the first ages, any sanction for such pretensions, I soon discovered that though, even then, some abuses of this worship had intruded themselves, the great teachers of Christian doctrine rebuked and denounced them as idolatrous: nor could there be given, perhaps, a more faithful exposition of all that the Catholics of the present day think and feel on this subject than is to be found in the following remarks which the great antagonist of heresies, Epiphanius, directed against some female heretics of his time by whom a more than due share of honour was paid to the Virgin:—"Her body (he says) was, I own, holy, but she was no God. She continued a Virgin, but she is not proposed for our adoration;—she herself adoring him who, having descended from heaven and the bosom of his Father, was born of her flesh. . . . . Though, therefore,

extravagances; but if the excess or perversion of a religious belief is to be assumed as an argument against the belief itself, far more vital points of faith than the intercessorial power of the Virgin may suffer by such logic.

she was a chosen vessel, and endowed with eminent sanctity, still she is a woman, partaking of our common nature, but deserving of the highest honours shown to the Saints of God.—She stands before them all on account of the heavenly mystery accomplished in her. But we adore no saint: and as this worship is not given to angels, much less can it be allowed to the daughter of Ann.—Let Mary, therefore, be honoured; but the Father, Son, and Holy Ghost alone be adored: let no one adore Mary."—*Adv. Collyridianos** *Hær.* 59.

Precisely such, as I conceive, is the wide and essential distinction which a Catholic divine of our own days would draw between adoration and honour;—between the worship due only to God, and that devout veneration which, in common with all Christian antiquity,

---

* These heretics, who were chiefly women, used to offer up to the Virgin a particular kind of cake, or bun, called in Greek *Collyris*. Their grand offering, however, was a loaf, which, at a stated season of the year, they presented to her with much solemnity, and then each of them partook of the oblation. In this ceremony the women performed the office of Priesthood.

we should offer to her whom an inspired voice pronounced " Blessed among women," and "the Mother of the Lord."

In short, looking back from the point where I had now arrived to the whole course and results of my search through those ages, I found myself forced to confess, that the Popery of the nineteenth century differs in no respect from the Christianity of the third and fourth; and that if St. Ambrose, St. Basil, and a few more such " flowers of Churches," had been able to borrow the magic nightcaps of their contemporaries, the Seven Sleepers, and were now, after a nap of about fifteen centuries, just opening their eyes in the town of Carlow, they would find in the person of Dr. Doyle, the learned Bishop of Leighlin and Ferns, not only an Irishman whose acquaintance even *they* might be proud to make, but a fellow Catholic every iota of whose creed would be found to correspond exactly with their own.

CHAPTER IX.

Prayers for the Dead.—Purgatory.—Penitential discipline.—Confession.—Origen.—St. Ambrose.—Apostrophe to the Shade of Father O'H * *.

AMONG those articles of Popery which I have enumerated as pre-existing in the creed of the Primitive Church, there are two, rather implied than mentioned, namely, a belief in Purgatory and auricular Confession, concerning which I have to offer a few brief remarks.

The solemn usage of praying for the Dead can be founded only on the belief that there exists a middle state of purification and suffering through which souls pass after death, and from which the prayers of the faithful may aid in delivering them. The antiquity, therefore, of the use of Prayers for the Dead (and we trace them through all the most ancient Liturgies) sufficiently prove to us how ancient was the belief on which they are founded. From the Second Book of the Maccabees (taking these Books merely in the Protestant view of them, as an uncanonical but authentic record) we learn that the ancient Jews, on this point, held the same faith as the Catholics:—" It is therefore a holy and a wholesome thought to pray for the dead, that they may be loosed from their sins."

We cannot wonder that such a belief should be thus ancient, for assuredly none can be more natural; nor, on the other hand, can any thing be less consistent either with our knowledge of *human* nature, or our notions of the *divine*, than such an absence of all gradation, both in reward and punishment, as the want of an intermediate state between heaven and hell must imply. What the Protestant divine, Paley, has said on the subject of Purgatory appears to me to be founded on such sentiments as both reason and nature approve: " Who can bear," he asks, " the thought of dwelling in everlasting torments? Yet who can say that a God everlastingly just will not inflict them? The mind of man seeks for some resource: it finds one only in conceiving *that some temporary punishment, after death, may purify the soul from its moral pollutions, and make it at last acceptable even to a Deity infinitely pure.*"

Fully agreeing with Paley on this point, it was with some pleasure I now discovered that, from Justin Martyr down to Basil and Ambrose, all the Fathers of the four first ages concur in opinion as to the existence of such an intermediate state;—the greater number of them interpreting a remarkable passage of St. Paul (1 Cor. iii. 13, 14, 15) as denoting expressly some region of purgation for the soul, where "the fire shall try every man's work of what sort it is," and where, as Origen explains the passage, "each crime shall, in proportion to its character, experience a just degree of punishment." Referring to the same passage of the Apostle, St. Ambrose says, "From hence it may be collected, that the same man is saved in part, and is condemned in part;" and, again, in a Commentary on this Epistle, he remarks:—"The

Apostle said 'He shall be saved, yet so as by fire,' in order that his salvation be not understood to be without pain. He shows that he shall be saved indeed, but that he shall undergo the pain of fire, and be thus purified; not like the unbelieving and wicked man who shall be punished in everlasting fire."—*Comment. in* 1 *Ep. ad Cor.* With similar views it was maintained by St. Hilary (and Origen seems to have been of the same opinion) that, after the day of Judgment, all—even the Blessed Virgin herself—must alike pass through this fire, to purify them from their sins.

The system of Penitential Discipline*, of which Confession forms one of the most im-

---

* As, in this world, the abuse of all good gifts follows as naturally on their use as shadows do on lights, it can little surprise us to find that the Sacrament of Penance was as much perverted from its true intention and spirit by the weak Catholics of other days, as it is, and will be, perverted by the same description of Catholics to the end of time. The existence of such false notions of Penance, in his own days, is thus noticed and reprehended by St. Ambrose:—" There are some who ask for penance, that they may be at once restored to communion. These

portant parts, was, as we learn from the ecclesiastical historian, Socrates, observed by the Bishops of Rome from the very earliest times; and the public penance of the Emperor Theodosius, in the great Church of Milan, proves what deference continued to be paid to the same spiritual ordinance, after Christianity had become the established religion of the Empire. Far different, however, were the notions of Repentance prevailing among the early Christians from those that have since been taught by the Apostles of the Reformation, who, in abolishing Confession, Penitential Fasting, &c. and getting rid of all that slow, humbling process of self-accusation and penance, by which the Catholic Church has,

do not so much desire to be loosed as to bind the Priest, for they do not unburden their own consciences, but they burden his. . . . Thus you may see persons walking about in white garments, who ought to be in tears for having defiled that colour of grace and innocence. Others there are who, provided they abstain from the Holy Sacraments, fancy they are doing penance. Others, while they have this in view, conclude they are licensed to sin, not aware that penance is the remedy, not the provocative of sin."—*De Pœnit. l. 2, c. 9.*

through all ages, disciplined her erring children, seem to have thought of little else than consulting the comfort of the sinner, and rendering his road to salvation short and easy. " There is yet," says Origen, "a more severe and arduous pardon of sin by penance, when the sinner washes his couch with his tears, and when he blushes not to disclose his sin to the Priest of the Lord, and to ask a remedy [*]. Thus is fulfilled what the Apostle says, ' Is any man sick among you, let him bring in the Priests of the Church.' (James, v. 14.)"

Of St. Ambrose it is said, by his secretary and biographer, that " as often as any one, in doing penance, confessed his faults to him, he wept so as to draw tears from the sinner. He seemed to take part in every act of sorrow. But, as to the occasions or causes of the crimes which they confessed, these he revealed to no one but God, with whom he interceded; leaving this good example to

---

[*] St. Augustin also writes: " Our merciful God wills us to confess in this world that we may not be confounded in the other."—*Hom.* 20.

his successors in the Priesthood, that they should be intercessors with God, not accusers before men."—*Paulin. in Vita Ambros.* The writings, indeed, of that age abound with affecting remarks upon the sacred and delicate duty which a Confessor has to perform, and the consoling balm he may apply to wounded and repentant spirits. " Show me bitter tears (says St. Gregory of Nyssa) that I may mingle mine with yours. Impart your trouble to the Priest, as to your Father; he will be touched with a sense of your misery. Show to him what is concealed, without blushing;— open the secrets of your soul, as if you were showing to a physician a hidden disorder; he will take care of your honour and of your cure."—*Serm. de Pœnit.*

How often, in reading such passages, did I call to mind my own innocent and Popery-believing days, when, as the regular season for Confession returned, I used to set off, early in the morning, to —— street Chapel, trembling all over with awe at the task that was before me, but still firmly resolved to tell the worst, without disguise. How vividly do I even, at this moment, remember kneeling down by the Confessional, and feeling my heart beat quicker, as the sliding-panel in the side opened, and I saw the meek and venerable head of the kind Father O'H—— stooping down to hear my whispered list of sins. The paternal look of the old man,— the gentleness of his voice, even in rebuke,— the encouraging hopes he gave of mercy as the sure reward of contrition and reformation,— all these recollections came freshly over my mind, as I now read the touching language employed by some of the Fathers on this subject; language such as the following, from the Homilies of Origen, which, though written when Christianity was little more than 200 years old, is as applicable to many a Catholic Confessor of our own times, as if indited but yesterday. " Only let the sinner carefully consider to whom he should confess his sin, what is the character of the physician;—if he be one who will be weak with the weak, who will weep with the sorrowful, and who understands the discipline of condolence and fellow-feeling: so that when his skill shall be known, and his pity felt, you may follow what he shall advise."—*Homil. 2. in Psalm. 27.* " If we discover our sins, not only to God, but to those who may thus apply a remedy to our wounds and iniquities, our sins will be effaced by him who said, ' I have blotted out thy iniquities as a cloud, and thy sins as a mist.' "—*Homil. 17. in Lucam.*

Shade of my revered Pastor, couldst thou have looked down upon me, in the midst of my folios, how it would have grieved thy meek spirit to see the humble little visitor of thy confessional,—him whom sometimes thou hast doomed, for his sins, to read the Seven Penitential Psalms daily,—to see him forgetting so soon the docility of those undoubting days, and setting himself up, God help him, as controvertist and Protestant!

CHAPTER X.

The Eucharist.—A glimpse of Protestantism.—Type, Figure, Sign, &c.—Glimpse lost again.—St. Cyril of Jerusalem.—St. Cyprian.—St. Jerom.—St. Chrysostom.—Tertullian.

In tracing the doctrines of Popery through the third and fourth ages, I have reserved, as may have been remarked, one of the most important of them all,—that relating to the Eucharist,—for separate consideration; and this I have done not merely on account of the great importance of the doctrine itself, but because on this point alone could I at all flatter myself with having discovered any little glimmerings of that Protestant Christianity of which I was in search.

The two first centuries, I saw clearly, must be given up as desperate; the language employed upon this subject by Ignatius, Justin Martyr, and Irenæus, having abundantly convinced me that, in those apostolic times, the literal or Popish interpretation of the words " This is my body " was the accepted doctrine; and that the Christians of the Primitive Church believed not only in the Real, corporal Presence, but in the miraculous change of substance after consecration. In the present depressed state of my hopes, however,—lowered as they were to the freezing temperature,—I would have compounded gladly for a sample of Protestantism even of a much less ancient date; and it was therefore with considerable satisfaction I had discovered in some writers of the third century the use of such expressions, in speaking of the Eucharist, as " Type," " Antitype," " Figure," &c., which seemed to afford a sort of escape from the difficulties of a Real Presence into the vague and figurative substitute for that miracle which, on the principle of believing " made easy," has been adopted by Protestants.

My self-gratulation, however, on this discovery was but of very short duration. In the first place, I soon found that this use of the words "Type," "Antitype," "Sign," &c. is not confined to those few Fathers to whom the Protestants look up as authority, but that the same terms have been also applied to the Eucharist by several of those writers whose real opinions respecting the nature of that Sacrament are known to have been as transubstantiatory as Popish heart could desire. Thus the great Catechist, Cyril of Jerusalem, who, in his doctrine concerning the Real Presence, goes the full lengths of all that Rome has ever asserted on the subject, yet applies to the Eucharist the word "Type," and that in a manner which seems to bear out the opinions of those who think that the term, as thus employed by the Fathers, denoted but the external appearance, or *accidents,* of the Eucharistic elements. "In the type of bread (says Cyril) is given to thee the body, and in the type of wine is given to thee the blood*." In the same manner, in one of those Liturgies

---

* Εν τυτω γαρ αρτου διδοται σοι σωμα και εν τυτω οινου διδοται σοι αιμα.

which go under the name of St. Basil, we find the bread and wine offered under the name of Antitypes, while in the prayer that follows, the Holy Spirit is invoked to come down and bless the gifts and "*make** the bread the body and the wine the blood of Christ."

If we may rely, indeed, on the authenticity of a passage, adduced by Bullinger from some MS. writings of Origen,—and I see no reason to doubt the honesty of the Reformer, in this instance,—it would appear, that Origen foresaw the heresy that was likely to arise on this point, and thus, by referring to the direct words of our Saviour, endeavoured to guard against it.—"He did not say (observes Origen) 'this is a symbol,' but 'this is a body;'—indicating thereby that nobody must suppose it to be a type†." Another passage, still more strongly to the same

---

* Αναδειξαι, which, as Suicerus acknowledges, signifies here to *render*, or *make*.

† Ου γαρ ειπε τουτο εστι συμβολον, αλλ' τουτο εστι σωμα· δεικτικως, ινα μη νομιζη τις τυπον ειναι.

purport, is quoted by the same eminent Protestant, Bullinger, from the writings of Magnes, a Priest of Jerusalem, who flourished in the third century:—" The Eucharist is not a *type* of the body and blood, as some men, defective in their understanding, have babbled, but rather *the* body and blood*."

But, whatever may be thought of the authenticity of these passages, I found, to my sorrow, that the Catholic view of the matter did not want the aid of any such questionable authorities. So far, indeed, from considering the Eucharist to be, itself, merely typical or symbolical, the early Christians, on the contrary, held it to be the accomplishment or reality of what *had* been but typical, under the Old Law. In the bread and wine offered by Melchisedek, the " Priest of the Most High God," they saw the figure or shadow of that Sacrifice which was to be instituted, from the same elements, in the Eucharist,—the type,

---

* Ουκ ιστιν Ευχαριστια τυπος του σωματος και του αιματος, ωσπερ τινες ερραψωδησαν πεπηρωμενοι τον νουν, μαλλον δε σωμα και αιμα.—*Advers. Theosthenem.*

in short, of that great mystery of which the Eucharist is the reality and the verity. "That the blessing given to Abraham (says Cyprian) might be properly celebrated, the representation of the Sacrifice of Christ, appointed in bread and wine, preceded it; which our Lord, perfecting and fulfilling it, himself made offering of in bread and wine; and thus he, who is the plenitude, fulfilled the truth of the prefigured image." *(Ep. 63, ad Cecilium.)*—Conceiving the show-bread of the Temple to have been also a prefiguration of the Eucharist, St. Jerom says, "There is as much difference betwixt the loaves offered to God in the Old Law and the body of Jesus Christ, as betwixt the shadow and the body, betwixt the image and the truth." *(Comment. in Ep. ad Tit.)*

It having been evidently the belief of the early orthodox Christians that the Eucharist had been prefigured in the offerings of the Old Law, to assert that they held this sacrament itself to be typical is to impute to them the absurdity of saying that it is but a type of types, a mere shadow of shadows*;—thus sinking their estimate of the importance of

* In a certain sense, and as far as it does not affect or qualify the belief in a Real Presence, the Catholic may with perfect consistency apply the words Figure or Symbol to the Eucharist, seeing that every sacrament, as such, must be an outward sign, and consequently a Figure or Symbol. In this sense it is that Pascal understands the terms in question, used by the Fathers; and as the view taken by so great a man of an article of faith so disputed cannot but be interesting, I shall here transcribe his own characteristically clear words:—" Nous croyons que la substance du pain étant changée en celle du corps de notre Seigneur Jésus Christ, il est présent réellement au Saint Sacrement. Voilà une des vérités. Une autre est que ce Sacrement est aussi une figure de la croix et de la gloire, et une commémoration des deux. Voilà la foi Catholique, qui comprend ces deux vérités qui semblent opposées.

" L'hérésie d'aujourd'hui, ne concevant pas que ce Sacrement contient tout ensemble, et la présence de Jésus Christ et sa figure, et qu'il soit Sacrifice, et Commémoration de Sacrifice, croit qu'on ne peut admettre l'une de ces vérités sans exclure l'autre.

" Par cette raison ils s'attachent à ce point, que ce Sacrement est figuratif; et en cela ils ne sont pas hérétiques. Ils pensent que nous excluons cette vérité; et de là vient qu'ils nous font tant d'objections sur les passages des Pères qui le disent. Enfin, ils nient la présence réelle; et en cela ils sont hérétiques."—*Pensees, Sec. Partie.*

this Institution to even a lower and more evanescent point of value than it has been reduced to by modern Sacramentarians and Arminians. That the very reverse, however, of all this was the case, I have just clearly shown; and how precious they held the assurance that, in place of the types and shadows of old, they had, in the Sacrifice of the New Law, a reality and a substance*, will appear from the language, ever glowing, of Chrysostom on this subject.—Asserting the Eucharist to be the accomplishment of the typical Passover, he says, " How much greater

* " We have an altar," says St. Paul, "whereof they have no right to eat which serve the tabernacle."—And yet (observes St. Thomas Aquinas on this passage) those who served the tabernacle had the *figure* of Jesus Christ in their Sacrifices. Where, then, would be the advantage that the Law of Grace professes to have over the Synagogue? If the Manna of the desert and the Eucharist are both alike but the *image* of his body, wherefore does the Saviour mark out that essential difference between them that the former was but a food miraculously formed in the air which gave not life, while the latter is "the bread which cometh from heaven," and which if any man eat of, "he shall live for ever." (John, vi.)—*See Conférences sur les Mystères*, tom. 2, p. 279.

holiness becomes thee, oh! Christian, who hast received greater symbols than the Holy of Holies contained;—for you have not the Cherubim but the Lord of the Cherubim dwelling in you;—you have not the Urn, and the Manna, and the Tables of Stone, and the Rod of Aaron, but the body and blood of our Lord." *(In Psalm.* 133.*)* Again, *Hom.* 46, he says—" This blood, even in the type, washed away sin. If it had so great power in the type,—if Death were so affrighted by the shadow, tell how it must be affrighted at the Verity itself. Truly tremendous are the mysteries of the Church; truly tremendous are our altars!"

The truth is, that the use of the words Type, Figure, Sign, &c., as applied to the Eucharist, is to be found neither in the Scriptures, nor in any of the pure Christian writers of the two first centuries. In the Scriptures, the Eucharistic elements are usually denoted by the words "body" and "blood;" and the same unqualified and unevasive language descended from the Apostles to their immediate successors in the Church; among whom, " to offer," " to receive," " to eat and drink the body and blood of Christ," were as familiar phrases as " to receive the Sacrament," or "to administer the Communion" are among ourselves.

With Tertullian may be said to have commenced that change in the public language of the Fathers on this subject,—that circumlocution, and, not unfrequently, ambiguity, in their notices of this mystery,—of which before there had been no example, and of which the Protestants have, in their despair, taken advantage as affording some shadow of plausibility to their arguments against the true Catholic doctrine of the Eucharist. The system of secresy to which such ambiguities and, as it would seem, inconsistencies in these holy writers may be traced, forms too remarkable a feature in the annals of the early Church, and is, indeed, too closely connected with the history of this and other Christian doctrines, to be dismissed without receiving some further consideration.

CHAPTER XI.

Discipline of the Secret.—Concealment of the Doctrine of the Real Presence.—St. Paul.—St. Clement of Alexandria.—Apostolical Constitutions.—System of secresy, when most observed.

THE system to which I have referred, at the close of the preceding chapter, as being the principal cause of that restraint and ambiguity which are observable in the language of some of the Fathers concerning the Eucharist, is well known among the learned by the name of the Discipline of the Secret, and by many is supposed to have been of apostolic origin. Among those alleged imitations of the religious policy of the Pagans with which the Primitive Christians and the Papists have alike been reproached, one of the most striking, as regards the former, is that distinction drawn in the early Church between the initiated and the non-initiated,—or, in other words, the baptized and the unbaptized,—and the sacred care with which the latter of these two classes were excluded from all knowledge of those more recondite and awful doctrines of the Faith, in which (to use the language of the Apostle) " the wisdom of God in a mystery" lies concealed.

In like manner, too, as among the Heathen Initiations, there were certain stages through which the candidate had to pass, not only for the purposes of discipline and instruction, but to stimulate also his ardour in the pursuit, before he arrived at the full and crowning close of his task, so in these Mysteries of the Church, and declaredly for the same reasons, a series of gradations was established through which the Catechumens and Penitents were obliged slowly to advance to that highest station where they were at length thought worthy of being initiated into the Faith, and the great Mystery, the Eucharist, was for the first time communicated to them. Till this period, not only were the Catechumens prohibited from being present at the celebration of that Sacrament, but all notion of its nature was carefully withheld from them, nor was it ever suffered to be mentioned, except obscurely, in their presence.

The chief object of all this secresy was to guard from the profaning scoffs of the infidel such doctrines as the ear of Faith was alone worthy to listen to; and the authority alleged for its adoption was no less sacred a one than the injunction of Christ himself:—" Place not holy things before dogs, nor pearls before swine." That the Apostles, in their capacity of " Stewards of the Mysteries of God," observed a similar rule of secresy was the current opinion of the Fathers; and the words of St. Paul (1 Cor. iii. 1, 2.) are often adduced by them to prove that already, in his time, this distinction between the Catechumens and the Faithful was in force. " And I, brethren, could not speak unto you as unto spiritual but as unto carnal persons, even as unto babes in Christ. I have fed you with milk and not with meat, for hitherto ye were not able to bear it; neither yet now are ye able."

" If, therefore (says St. Clement of Alexandria, in commenting on this passage), Milk be said by the Apostle to belong to babes, and Meat to them that are perfect, Milk will be understood to be *Catechizing*, as the first kind of food of the soul, but Meat the *concealed Theorics*." How strongly St. Jerom also was of opinion that St. Paul acted upon this principle appears from his reply to his friend Evagrius, who had consulted him respecting the meaning of an obscure passage of the Apostle with regard to the sacrifice of Melchisedek:—" You are not to suppose (says St. Jerom) that Paul could not easily have explained himself; but the time was not come for such explanation. He sought to persuade the Jews, and not the Faithful, to whom the mystery might have been delivered without reserve."

Did the curious Collection, known by the name of the Apostolical Constitutions, possess any such claim to a rank among scriptural writings as Whiston labours to establish for it, the apostolic origin of the Discipline of the

Secret could be no longer doubtful;—these Constitutions having been professedly collected, under such a law of secresy, by the fellow-labourer of St. Paul, Clement, as he is himself thus made to declare:—" The Constitutions, dedicated to you, the Bishops, by me, Clement, in Eight Books;—which it is not fitting to publish before all, because of the Mysteries contained in them."

But, though the authenticity claimed by Whiston, with such profuse waste of learning, for this book, be now generally disallowed, the work still furnishes a proof that, in the third or fourth century when it was fabricated, a belief prevailed that those unwritten traditions and doctrines over which the Church drew a veil of silence had descended to her, under the same religious law of secresy, from the Apostles themselves. " We receive," says St. Basil, " the dogmas transmitted to us by writing, and those which have descended to us from the Apostles, beneath the veil and mystery of oral tradition. . . . . . . The Apostles and Fathers who prescribed from the beginning certain rites to the Church, knew how to preserve the dignity of the Mysteries by the secresy and silence in which they enveloped them. For what is open to the ear and the eye is no longer mysterious. For this reason several things have been handed down to us without writing, lest the vulgar, too familiar with our dogmas, should pass from being accustomed to them to the contempt of them."—*De Spirit. Sanct. c. 27.*

Upon the controversy which is known to have been maintained among the learned as to the precise time when the Discipline of the Secret was first introduced into the Church, it is not my intention here to dwell. Some, as we have seen, trace its origin as far back as the time of the Apostles[*], while others suppose it to have been first practised towards the close of the second century, and others, again, contrary to all authority, date its com-

---

[*] Among moderns, Schelstrate has contended most strenuously for the apostolic origin of the Secret, while, in opposition to him, Tentzelius and others refer its rise to about the close of the second century.

mencement so low down as the fourth. The truth seems to be that the *principle* of this policy was acted upon, in the Christian Church, from its very beginning. So strongly has not only St. Paul, but our Saviour himself, inculcated a sacred reserve in promulgating the Mysteries of the Faith, that there can be no doubt the succeeding teachers of the Church would, in this, as in all things else, follow their Divine Master's precept.

But though, as a principle, this reverential guard over the Mysteries was observed, doubtless, from the very first rise of Christianity, it does not appear to have been strictly enforced, as a rule of discipline, till about the close of the second century. The curiosity and, still more, the bitter enmity excited by the rapid spread of a religion founded wholly, as it appeared, on mysteries, but whose progress was, in unbelieving eyes, the greatest mystery of all, rendered increased caution necessary on the part of its ministers; and the divine precept by which they were enjoined to hide the " holy things" of the

Faith from unbelievers began, about this time, to be acted upon by them with a degree of jealous strictness proportionate to the prying insolence and violence by which they were encompassed.

CHAPTER XII.

Doctrine of the Trinity.—St. Justin.—Irenæus.—Apparent heterodoxy of the Fathers of the Third Century.—Accounted for by the Discipline of the Secret.—Tertullian, Origen, Lactantius, &c.

It has been asserted by more than one learned writer, that the doctrine of the Trinity was not included among the mysteries to which the protection of this rule of secresy was extended*. But such an assumption is not only inconsistent with the main objects for which such a rule was established, but is also, as it will not be difficult to show, at variance with fact. It was, indeed, the pious horror

---

* In defiance, as it appears to me, of all evidence, it has been maintained by Tentzelius, Casaubon and others, that it was neither the Trinity, nor any of the other dogmas of the Faith, but merely the rites and ceremonies of the two Sacraments of Baptism and the Eucharist that were intended to be concealed from the non-initiated by the observance of this Discipline.

of exposing such high mysteries as that of the
Trinity to the scoffs and, what was still worse,
the misrepresentations of the Gentiles, that
formed the chief motive of the Christian
Pastors for the policy which they adopted,
—a policy which, on some points (such as that
of the Seven Sacraments*), is supposed to
have led them to preserve an unbroken silence,
but which, for the most part, consisted in
holding such language respecting any mystery
they had to mention before unbelievers, as
was, at the same time, transparent enough to

---

* It is to the operation of the Discipline of the Secret that Catholic writers attribute the entire silence which they acknowledge has been preserved, on the subject of the Seven Sacraments, in all the authentic monuments of antiquity that remains to us. According to Schelstrate,— one of those by whom the circumstance is thus accounted for,—it is not till the seventh century that any mention of the Seven Sacraments occurs:—" Si pervolvamus omnia antiquitatis monumenta, si perscrutemur cuncta antiquissimorum Patrum scripta, si investigemus ipsa Synodorum decreta, nullum librum, nullum decretum reperiri, quod ante septimum sæculum egerit de Septem Sacramentis, eorumque ritus exposuerit."—*Schelstraten. De Disciplin. Arcan.*

allow the truth to shine out to the initiated, and yet too obscure to betray either the teacher or his doctrines to the profane. In this reserved and ambiguous manner do Tertullian and some of the succeeding Fathers speak of the Eucharist; and still more evasively, from the same cause, have almost all the Fathers of the first three centuries and a half spoken of the Trinity.

This latter fact I am, in a peculiar degree, anxious to impress on the reader; seeing that it is of importance to my subject to show that by an almost exactly similar fate has the progress of these two mysteries, the Trinity and the Real Presence, been all along marked; and that the same cause which produced, in some of the early Fathers, that ambiguity of language, on the subject of the Eucharist, of which the Protestants have availed themselves for the support of their schism, produced also that still greater ambiguity and inconsistency in the language of the same Fathers, respecting the Trinity, which has, with a similar degree of dexterity, been employed, in favour of their own heresy, by the Arians.

I have already remarked how much more free from the restraints of this singular Discipline were those writers who flourished previous to the close of the second century than were any of their successors for the next hundred and fifty years; and I need but mention, in proof of this fact, that the same illustrious Father, St. Justin, who, as I have shown, ventured, in his Address to the Sovereign and Princes of the Empire, to promulgate the doctrine of Transubstantiation, proclaimed also, in the same public document, the mystic dogma of the Trinity.

How far the circumstance of his not being an ecclesiastic may have rendered this Father somewhat less guarded in his public writings, I will not pretend to determine; but it is plain that even he thought it prudent so far to disguise or soften down some of the more salient points of the doctrine of the Trinity as to present it to the minds of unbelievers in its least startling shape. Knowing well that the charge of Polytheism was lying in wait for him, as well from Jews as from Gentiles, he refrains most cautiously, in his Apology, from asserting the co-eternity of the Son with the Father, and even, in some passages, expressly declares the inferior nature of the former:— "*Next after God*, we adore and love that Word which is derived from the ineffable and unbegotten God." And again, in speaking of the Logos, "Than whom a more Royal and just Ruler, *after God the Father*, we know not one."

The charge of heterodoxy which such language has drawn down upon St. Justin would appear not to be without some foundation, had we not the Discipline of the Secret to account for it satisfactorily, and did there not occur other passages, in the very same document, where this veil of reserve is withdrawn and the true doctrine disclosed to the Initiate. Of this nature is the following, showing clearly that the pure, orthodox belief,—that which holds the Son to have been generated, not created, and to have been with the Father from all eternity,—was the belief delivered to

St. Justin, and by him taught to the baptized:—" But his Son, who alone is properly called his Son, the Word, who was with him and was begotten by him before the Creatures."

Another writer of the same age, Irenæus, may be cited as yet more remarkable for the extent to which he has ventured to unveil both the Sacrifice in the Eucharist, and, still more fully, the great mystery of the Eternal Generation of the Son. With so much bolder a hand than any of his successors has he laid open the depths of this latter doctrine, that in him alone does Whiston allow that there can be found any sanction for that high view of the Trinity, to which Whiston himself was opposed; but which, however apparently, at times, "shorn of its beams," has been, throughout every age of the Church, her unchanging doctrine. It was from want of attention to the operation of the Discipline of the Secret that Whiston and others have been led into exactly the same error, respecting the Trinity, that other Protestant divines have fallen into, on the subject of the Real corporal Presence.

Far different, indeed, from the language of

Justin and Irenæus was that held, on both these dogmas, by the Fathers of the following age, when the system of secresy had begun strictly to be acted upon, and when, amidst the storms of persecution that gathered round their heads, the ministers of the Faith found in this holy Silence a protection both for their doctrines and themselves. Nothing, in truth, can show more strongly the difference that, in this respect, distinguished the two periods, than a comparison of the conduct of St. Justin with that of St. Cyprian, in situations very nearly similar. The former, as we have seen in his Defence of Christianity, addressed to the Princes of the Empire, did not hesitate so far to throw open the sanctuary of the Faith as to place before them its two great Arcana, the Trinity and the Real Presence; whereas St. Cyprian, when, in like manner, called upon to stand forth in vindication of his religion, ventured no further, in his public Epistle on the occasion, than to assert the doctrine of the Unity of God, leaving the Trinity and the mystic Sacraments of the Church wholly unmentioned.

So cautiously, indeed, are the Christians of Cyprian's age known to have shrunk from all mention of the Trinity before the uninitiated, that, in reviewing the Acts of the Martyr, St. Pontius, the chief point on which the learned Schelstrate rests his conviction of their spuriousness is their representing this Martyr as speaking openly of the Trinity before the emperors Philip, while still Gentiles,—a violation of the law of secresy, on this subject, of which no Christian would, at that time*, have been likely to be guilty.

Were we to form our judgment solely on some detached passages of Tertullian, Origen, and Lactantius, we must either come to Whiston's conclusion that the present accepted doctrine of the Trinity was not that of the primitive Church; or else suppose that the truth of this divine mystery, having broken

* There occur also some instances of the same strict observance of secresy, in the second century. Thus, we find, Alexander, the Martyr, when preaching to the prisoners, made no mention of the Holy Spirit, nor of the mystery of the Trinity; and when ordered by Aurelius to explain all the dogmas of his faith, answered that he was not permitted by Christ to place holy things before dogs.

out brightly and genuinely in the writings of St. Justin and Irenæus, was again, for an interval of a hundred and fifty years, eclipsed and lost. To give but an instance or two of the imperfect views, respecting the relation between Christ and God, which the Fathers of the third century suffered to glimmer through their writings, we find the following unorthodox passage in Tertullian on the subject:—" God was not always a Father or Judge, since he could not be a Father before he had a Son, nor a Judge before there was any sin; and there was a time when both sin and the Son were not."

The fear of drawing upon themselves the imputation of Polytheism from the Gentiles appears to have been one of the chief motives with these holy men for their reserve respecting the Trinity; and how readily disposed were not only the Pagans, but some of the heretics, to found such an accusation on this doctrine appears from the account given by Tertullian of the Sabellians of his day, whose first question, as he tells us, in meeting any of the orthodox, was "Well, my friends, do we believe in one God or three?" It was evidently to counteract such an impression that St. Cyprian, as we have seen, in his Letter to the Proconsul of Africa, contented himself with solely establishing the Unity of God; and that another learned Father, Lactantius, about half a century later, thought it prudent to put forth the following declaration:—"Our Saviour taught that there is but one God, and that he alone is to be worshipped; nor did he ever say once himself that he was God. For, he had not been faithful to his trust, if, when he was sent to take away Polytheism, and assert the Unity of God, he had introduced another besides the one God. This had been not to preach the doctrine of one God, nor to do the business of him that sent him, but his own."—*De vera Sapient.*

In a similar manner, with the view of removing those prejudices which were known to exist against Christianity, from a notion that, like Paganism, it sanctioned the worship of many Gods, we find Origen, in his Treatise on Prayer, going so far as almost to deny that Christ is to be considered an object of supplication or thanksgiving:—" But if we understand (says this Father) what Prayer is, care must be taken that no derivative Being be the object of Prayer,—no, not Christ himself, but only the God and Father of the Universe, to whom also our Saviour himself prayed, as we have before expounded, and as he teaches us to pray. For, when one said to him, Teach us to pray, he does not teach us to pray to himself, but to his Father, saying ' Our Father which art in heaven.' "

It is from attending solely to passages such as these that not only calumniators of the Fathers, like Daillé and Jurieu, but even Catholics of distinguished character, such as Petau and Huet*, have been led into the error of accusing the teachers of the early Church of Arianism; whereas, a little more fairness in

---

* This learned Catholic, in referring to the heretical opinions which are to be found in such passages as I have above cited from the Fathers, doubts whether to impute them to impiety or unskilfulness. But the self-imposed restraint under which they, at times, wrote affords the true clue to all such difficulties.

some of the theologians just named, and a little more industry in the others, would have enabled them to cite from writings of the very same Fathers,—writings produced under circumstances that left them more free to unfold the mysteries of their Faith,—passages fully asserting the dogma of the Tri-une Deity, in all its primitive, orthodox, and inscrutable grandeur. Thus Tertullian who, as we have seen, in addressing the Stoic Hermogenes, could so far shrink from the true exposition of this doctrine as to declare that there was a time when God was not a Father, and had not a Son, has yet, in his Defence of the Trinity against Praxeas, given conclusive evidence of his belief in the in-dwelling of the Word with God from all eternity; and has, moreover, in one sentence, defined the consubstantial union of the Three Persons as strictly as was afterwards done by Athanasius himself, —calling it "Una substantia in tribus cohærentibus." In a like manner, too, Origen, notwithstanding passages such as I have above cited from him, which lower our Saviour in the scale of Being to a rank secondary and derivative, has asserted so orthodoxly, in other parts of his writings, the co-equality of the Son, in Godship, with the Father, as to have drawn from Bishop Bull, the defender of the Nicene Anathema, the praise of perfect orthodoxy.

The natural working, indeed, of the wary policy which gave to these writers such an appearance of inconsistency, may be traced visibly through the course of the writings of St. Clement of Alexandria, in some of the earlier of which the equality of the Son to the Father is expressly maintained*; while, in his subsequent works, whether yielding to prudence, or to that admiration of the occult wisdom of the Greeks which he so warmly avows†, he withdraws this bolder view of the nature of

---

* His words are, if I recollect right, ἐξισωθεὶς τῷ πατρί.

† In citing the words of St. Paul, "We speak the wisdom of God in a mystery, even the hidden mystery," Clement remarks that the Holy Apostle here observes "the prophetic and really ancient concealment, from whence the excellent doctrines of the Grecian philosophers were derived to them."

the Redeemer, and represents him, almost invariably, as a subordinate and created Being.

That this reserve and ambiguity on the subject of the Trinity continued to be practised to as late a period as the middle of the fourth century appears from the following remarkable passage, in one of the Catecheses of St. Cyril of Jerusalem, which is in itself confirmatory of my view of the whole system:—" *We do not declare the Mysteries concerning the Father, Son, and Holy Ghost to a Heathen; nor do we speak plainly to the Catechumens about those Mysteries.* But we say many things often in an occult way, that the Faithful who know them may understand them; and that those who do not understand them may not be hurt thereby."

CHAPTER XIII.

Doctrine of the Incarnation.—Importance attached to it by Christ himself.—John, vi.—Ignatius.—Connexion between the Incarnation and the Real Presence.—Concealment of the latter doctrine by the Fathers.—Proofs of this concealment.

HAVING dwelt thus long upon the influence which that rule of policy, called the Discipline of the Secret, exercised so manifestly over the writings of the Fathers on the subject of the Trinity, I shall now proceed to show that the same influence,—though certainly, in many instances, to a much less considerable degree, —affected the public writings of these same Fathers, on the no less vital and mysterious doctrine of the Eucharist.

It may be observed to have been chiefly round those points of belief on which the Christians felt themselves most exposed to the charge of borrowing from the theology of the Heathens that they took the most especial care to throw the protection of this sacred silence. Of this description was, as I have already shown, the Trinity; and in the same predicament, as doctrines liable to be misrepresented, were the great mysteries of the Sonship and the Incarnation; the former of which the philosophic Gentiles exclaimed against, as originating in the same gross notions which had dictated the genealogy of the Heathen Gods; while, by such scoffers as Celsus, the Incarnation of the Eternal Word was compared to those transformations which Jupiter underwent in his multifarious love-adventures. In truth, the very first great point of the Christian scheme of Redemption which Christians themselves, in the presumptuous exercise of their judgment, dared to call into question, was the Incarnation of the Redeemer. Under the very eyes of our Lord himself there arose, as we have seen, a sect of heretics[*], who, refusing to believe that Spirit so pure could clothe itself in corrupt flesh, chose rather to

---

[*] The Docetæ. See page 17.

deny his humanity, and thus, in fact, nullify his mission as a Redeemer by removing that only link between the divine and human nature through which a mediation, implying sympathies with both, could be effected.

To obviate the mischiefs of this heresy,—coeval, as it would seem, with Christianity itself,—and confirm the truth of the manifestation of God in the Flesh was, it is evident, one of the most anxious objects, as well of our Saviour himself, as of those who acted under his authority. Had we no other proof, indeed, of the prevalence of such an error, respecting his nature, the solicitude he showed, in his interview with the Apostles after his resurrection, to convince them of his corporeality, by making them handle his limbs and by eating in their presence, would be sufficient to prove both the doubts, as to his humanity, that prevailed, and the immense importance which he himself attached to their removal: " Handle me (he says) and see; for a Spirit hath not flesh and bones, as ye see me have:" or, as he is made to say, in an apocryphal work, cited by Origen*, "I am not an incorporeal Demon."

In the First Epistle of St. John we find those heretics who denied the reality of Christ's body thus denounced:—"Every spirit that confesseth that Jesus Christ is come in the flesh is of God; and every spirit that confesseth not that Jesus Christ is come in the flesh is not of God; and this is that spirit of Antichrist whereof ye have heard that it should come; and even now already is it in the world." It is, indeed, supposed to have been principally with the view of obviating so dangerous an error that the same Apostle wrote his Gospel; and not only the earnestness with which he anathematizes this heresy in his Epistle, but also the pains taken by him, as Evangelist, to assure the world of the real death of Christ and of the issuing of real blood and water from his wounded side, render such a view of his design, in writing this sacred narrative, both natural and rational.

* The Doctrine of Peter.—*Origen. de Princip.*

It is, in fact, in the 6th chapter of his Gospel, —that remarkable chapter, whose testimony to the marvellous nature and virtues of the Eucharist the ingenuity of Protestant Divines so vainly labours to explain away,—that we find the very strongest proof of the vital importance attached, in the Christian scheme, to the establishment of the *verity* of Christ's flesh and blood. Nor can it be doubted that, as St. John's main object, in this Gospel, was to refute and extinguish that pernicious heresy which, by denying the reality of the flesh of Christ, would deprive mankind of the benefits of his Incarnation, so the stress which he here represents our Saviour as laying upon the ever blessed and life-giving effects of the Eucharist has evidently the same most momentous object in view,—showing emphatically that this miraculous Sacrament was, as it were, a sequel to the mystery of the Incarnation; and that the mighty privileges and benefits which the latter had procured for mankind were, by the former, to be perpetuated and commemorated through all time.

That such was the light in which our Saviour himself represented this Sacrament, in that memorable discourse uttered by him in the Synagogue, at Capernaüm, none but those who perversely wrest the word of God to their own rash judgments will venture to deny. "One principal motive," says a learned Protestant writer, "that modern Divines have to deny that John, vi. is to be taken of the Eucharist is this, viz. that the effects and consequences there attributed to the eating and drinking Christ's flesh and blood (especially that of eternal life and all evangelical blessings annexed to it) are too great and valuable to be applied to the Communion*."

Nothing can be more just or candid than this remark. Hence, in truth, all the wretched shifts resorted to by Church of England divines† for the purpose of robbing the

* *Johnson's Unbloody Sacrifice.*

† Thus, Dr. Whitby, adopting, in matter-of-fact seriousness, that allegorical and anagogical mode of interpretation, which Clement of Alexandria and Origen employed to mystify their hearers, had the conscience to maintain that by the phrases "eating his flesh" and "drinking

Catholic doctrine of the support of this chapter, and enabling the Protestant to sink

his blood," in John, vi., Christ meant nothing more than " believing his doctrines!" On this opinion Johnson remarks,—" It must be owned that if our Saviour, by men's eating his flesh and drinking his blood, meant nothing but so obvious a thing as receiving him and his doctrine by faith and obedience, he clothed his thoughts in most unnatural language;" and again, " We may as properly be said to eat and drink the Trinity by believing in it as to eat the body of Christ by bare faith."

Next came Bishop Hoadley, who, rejecting all application of John, vi. to the Eucharist whatever, described the discourse of our Saviour in the Synagogue as " only a very high figurative representation to the Jews then about him of their duty and obligation to receive to their hearts and digest his whole doctrine as the food and life of their souls." Dr. Waterland, who disapproved alike of Whitby's doctrinal interpretation and Hoadley's reduction of the Sacrament to a mere communicative Feast, is of opinion that the Chapter in question may be *applied* to the Eucharist, but not *interpreted* of it; and brings forward a theory of his own respecting " Spiritual Eating and Drinking," of the merits of which some judgment may be formed from the fact that, though disapproving of Whitby's notion of eating *doctrines*, he himself interprets a passage of St. Paul (Heb. xiii. 10.) to mean, eating *the Atonement!*—(*Review of the Doctrine of the Eucharist, p.* 145.) In order to get rid, too, of the testimony of St. Ignatius to the true meaning of John, vi., Dr. Water-

the miraculous character of the Eucharist down to the "low" view* taken of it by the Socinians and Hoadleyites. But the sense of all the great teachers of Christianity is against them; and, above all, of those earliest in the field of the Faith. The apostolical Ignatius, who had been the disciple of him " who wrote these things," and had doubtless heard, from the holy Penman's own lips, their true import and spirit, understood, manifestly, by the promise of Eternal Life conveyed on that occasion, no vaguely allegorical lesson of faith or doctrine, but a

land contends that this holy man, in speaking of his enjoyment of "the Bread of Life," had no reference whatever to the Eucharist in his thoughts, but, being then about to suffer martyrdom, was merely looking forward to the prospect of eating of Christ's Flesh, in the other world! p. 153. Such are the straits to which men are always sure to be driven who endeavour to make out a case where there is no case to be made.

* " If any person think this *a low character* of such a rite instituted by our Lord himself, upon so great and remarkable occasion," &c. &c.—*Bishop Hoadley, Plain Account of the Nature and End of the Sacrament of the Lord's Supper.*

clear assurance of a happy resurrection and immortality, to be derived from that communion with the body of Christ which is enjoyed by eating his flesh and drinking his blood in the Eucharist. Hence is it that the holy Ignatius speaks of this Sacrament, in language which no other part of Scripture, but this Chapter of John, justifies;—calling it, on the strength of the privileges and virtues there annexed to it, the Medicine of Immortality and Antidote against Death.

How perfectly the view taken of the Eucharist by the Catholics,—namely, that it was part and parcel of the mystery of the Incarnation,—was understood by the Gnostic Christians themselves, is evident from their conduct. For this reason was it that the Docetæ absented themselves, as we have seen, from public worship,— not that the sect, in general, entertained any objection to the Eucharist, according to their own Phantastic and spiritualizing view of it, but because they were unwilling to sanction, by joining in communion with the orthodox, that belief in the *reality* of the flesh present which the latter, it was known, maintained.

That the Fathers regarded this Sacrament in the same light,—viewing it not only as a continuance, but as an extension of the Incarnation*,—a great abundance of passages might be adduced to prove. Thus, for instance, St. Gregory of Nyssa draws a comparison between the two Mysteries:—" The body of Christ (says this Father) was, by the inhabitation of the *Word* of God, transmuted into a divine dignity, and so I now believe, that the bread sanctified by *the Word* of God is transmuted into the body of the Word of God. This bread, as the Apostle says, *is sanctified by the Word of God and prayer*, not that, as food, it passes into the body, but that it is instantly changed into the body of Christ, agreeably to what he said, This is my Body.

---

* By calling the Eucharist an extension of the Incarnation, they meant that while, in the latter mystery, Christ but joined himself to one individual nature, and to no one person, in the former he joins himself not only to all individual natures, but also to their very persons. " Eam quam idcirco Patres *Incarnationis extensionem* appellarunt. In illâ enim uni individuae naturae sese adjunxit, nulli personae; at in istâ se singulis individuis, imò etiam personis adjunx't."—*De Linguidcs Conciones de Sanctissimo Eucharistiæ Sacramento.*

And therefore does the Divine Word commix itself with the weak nature of man, that, by partaking of the divinity, our humanity may be exalted."

In like manner, we find St. Ambrose pointing out the same analogy between the deified flesh and the deified bread. After asserting the dogma of Transubstantiation, in its highest Catholic sense, he proceeds,—" We will now examine the truth of the mystery from the example itself of the Incarnation. Was the order of nature followed, when Jesus was born of a virgin? Plainly not. Then why is that order to be looked for here?" Many other passages, to the same purport, might be adduced from the Fathers: but it is needless to multiply citations. The very view taken by the early Christians of the miraculous change of the elements implies that they considered the Eucharist as a kindred mystery with that of the Incarnation;—as the wonderful means, in short, by which Christ perpetually renews his incarnate presence upon earth, and continues to feed his creatures with the same flesh by which he redeemed them.

CHAPTER XIV.

Concealment of the Doctrine of the Eucharist.—Proofs.—Calumnies on the Christians.—Protestant view of this Sacrament—*not* that taken by the early Christians.

WHEN so great, as we have seen, was the solicitude and watchfulness with which the Church screened from the eyes of the profane all her other great dogmas, with no less jealous care would she conceal, or, at least, soften down, through the medium of enigmatic language, a doctrine so mysterious and astounding as that of the Real Presence,—the test most trying of all (*next*, perhaps, to the Trinity) of that implicit faith, by which, as by its sheet-anchor, the whole Christian scheme of salvation holds. Accordingly, we are not only expressly told that this dogma was among the most hidden deposits of the Secret, but the language employed by the few Fathers who, in the third age, ventured to allude to it, shows with what sensitive caution they shrunk from any disclosure of its true nature. Thus Origen talks mysteriously and vaguely of "eating the offered breads, which by prayers *are made a certain holy body.*" St. Cyprian, too, in relating, with an awe that betrays his real belief, the miraculous circumstance of a warning having been given to some profaner of the Sacrament by a flame bursting forth from the box that held the consecrated bread, describes the box thus signalized, as "containing the *Holy Thing of the Lord.*"

Nothing, indeed, could show more strikingly both how awful were the associations with which they invested this mystery themselves, and how jealous was their fear lest it should become known to the infidel, than the language of another Father of this time, Tertullian, who, in representing to his wife the consequences of her marrying a Pagan after his death, says,—" You would, by marrying an infidel, thereby fall into this fault, that the Pagans would come to the knowledge of our mysteries. Will not your husband know what you taste *in secret*, before any other food; and, if he perceives bread, will he not imagine that it is what is so much spoken of?"—*Ad Uxorem, lib.* ii. *c.* 5. In the following century we find St. Basil alluding covertly to the Eucharist as "the Communion of *the Good Thing;*" and Epiphanius, when obliged to describe, before uninitiated hearers, the Institution of this Sacrament, thus slurs over the particulars of that astounding event: "We see that our Lord took a thing in his hands, as we read in the Gospel, that he rose from table, that he resumed the things, and having given thanks, he said, this is my somewhat."

Even St. Gregory of Nyssa, by whom the great miracle of the Metastoicheiosis, or Transubstantiation, is put forth more boldly and definitely than by almost any of his predecessors, yet, in one of his most explicit passages on the subject, and in a writing, too, intended expressly for the initiated, stops short, as if awe-struck, when about to mention the word "body," and leaves to the minds of his hearers to fill up the blank.—"These things he gives us by virtue of the blessing, changing the nature of the visible things into —that."

There can hardly, perhaps, be a better proof of the extreme secresy with which this mystery was guarded than that Arnobius, who was but a Catechumen when he wrote upon Christianity, had been kept in such ignorance of the use made of wine in this rite, that in a passage where he reproaches, if I recollect right, the Pagans, with their libations to the Deities, he tauntingly demands of them " What has God to do with wine * ?"

Still enough, notwithstanding this system of reserve and secresy, had transpired respecting the Christian doctrine of the Eucharist, to set the imagination and malevolence of unbelievers at work. Indistinct notions of dark, forbidden Feasts, where, it was said, flesh and blood were served up to the guests, became magnified by the fancies of the credulous into the most monstrous fictions. Stories were told and believed of the dreadful rites practised by the Christians in their Initiations;—of an

* " Quid Deo cum vino est?"

infant, covered with paste, being set before the new-comer, on which he was required to inflict the first murderous stab, and then partake of its flesh and blood with the rest, as their common pledge of secresy. It is not difficult, of course, to see, through all this disfigurement of calumny, the true doctrine of which the profane had caught these perverting glimpses.

By such monstrous imputations was it that some of the most cruel persecutions of the Christians were provoked and justified; and yet no power of cruelty, not the agonies of death itself, could wrest their secret from them. Had they seen nothing more in this sacrament than a simple type or memorial, such as the Arminian and Socinian consider it, they had but to say so, and not only persecution would have been thus foiled of its prey, but, what was of still dearer import to them, their creed would have won more ready acceptance. But no:—far more " hard to be understood" was the secret object of their worship; and, when asked, as they were frequently by the Pagans, " Why conceal what you adore?"

their answer might have been, with truth, "*Because* we adore it." They saw, as the Catholics see to this day, what insulting profanation such a doctrine is, in the hands of the incredulous, exposed to; in what mire of ridicule and blasphemy their "holy things" would be rolled; and accordingly, even when threatened with torments to extort from them their secret, they saw but one duty before them—to be silent, and die.

Had Christian antiquity bequeathed to us, on the subject of the Eucharist, no other evidence than this solemn and significant silence,—had we not also the ancient Liturgies of the Church, and the catechetical writings of her Fathers, to bear ample testimony to the Catholic doctrine, on this point,—there still would have been, in this very mystery and silence, abundant evidence to convince any reasoning mind, that the Protestant notion of the Eucharist could *not* have been that entertained by the Primitive Christians. The simple history, in short, of this doctrine's reception and progress, through all its earlier stages, would be more than sufficient for such a purpose. For, to maintain that a mystery which, on its first promulgation, startled our Lord's disciples themselves,—which the Gnostic heretics of the first age shrunk from, as involving the doctrine of the Incarnation,—which the Pagans, from some indistinct glimpses of its real nature, represented as a murderous repast, a feast of "abominable meats,"—which by the Priests themselves who administered it was seldom spoken of but as a "tremendous mystery," one to be guarded from the eyes of the infidel, at the price of life itself,—to assert, that the dread object of all this concealment and worship, this amazement, horror, adoration, alarm, was nothing more than a simple sign or memorial, a mere representation of our Saviour's body and blood under the symbols of bread and wine, a sacramental food in which Christ's presence is figurative, not real, and to which, therefore, consisting as it does of mere bread and wine, to offer up any adoration is an act of idolatry,— to expect to have it believed, for a moment, by any one who has at all inquired into the subject, that such and no more was the sense attached to this divine ordinance by the first Christians, is, on the part of the Protestants, I must say, a most gross and wholesale demand of that implicit faith, from others, of which they are so perilously sparing themselves.

When again, too, after contemplating all those awful circumstances which marked the reception and observance of this rite among mankind, we look back to the stupendous occasion on which it was first instituted; when we recollect the dreadful denunciations of the Apostle against such as, by irreverence to this Sacrament, are " guilty of the body and blood of the Lord," and remember that some, among the Corinthians, who " discerned not the Lord's body," were smitten by God with diseases and death*,—we cannot but marvel at the responsibility those Christians take upon themselves, who venture to cast off the ancient Faith, upon this most vital of its

* 1 Corinth. xi. 30.

doctrines; who, first, refining away our Saviour's solemn declaration on the subject*, dispose, in the same manner, of the Apostle's tremendous comment upon that text; and, in the very face of his denouncements against those who " *discern not the Lord's body*" in this Sacrament, venture deliberately to deny that the Lord's body is there!

* As the Reformer, Zuinglius, took the liberty of altering Christ's language, and reads " This *signifies* my body," so Bishop Hoadley, in like manner, presumes to supply a word which he thinks wanting, and makes it " This *I call* my body." It is remarkable enough, indeed, that Protestants who are so much for referring to the language of Scripture, on every occasion, should yet, in this important instance, question its most express and simple declaration, —a declaration repeated, in almost exactly the same words, by three of the Evangelists, as well as by St. Paul, and explained, exactly in the same sense, by our Saviour, in the discourse reported by St. John. " Unam perpetuò (says an obscure, but sensible writer) Scripturam clamitant; sed ubi ventum est ad eam, auditis quomodo legant. Tam aperta sunt verba; in omnibus Evangelistis sunt eadem. Omnia tamen pervertunt, omnia ad hæresim suum trahunt."

CHAPTER XV.

Concealment of the Eucharist—most strict in Third Century.—St. Cyprian—his timidity—favourite Saint of the Protestants.—Alleged proofs against Transubstantiation.—Theodoret.—Gelasius.—Believers in the Catholic Doctrine of the Eucharist, Erasmus, Pascal, Sir Thomas More, Fenelon, Leibnitz, &c.

FROM what I have said, in the preceding Chapter, of the system of mystery and restraint which the Fathers of the third and fourth centuries, but more particularly of the former, thought it politic to impose upon themselves in speaking of the Eucharist, it will not be deemed wonderful that there should occur passages in their public writings and discourses, which, being intended by them to be ambiguous, have fully attained that object; and that, designed originally as such passages were to veil the truth from the unbeliever and the heretic, they should, to eyes wilfully blind, still perform the same office.

The only wonder, indeed, is, taking all the circumstances we have here reviewed into consideration, that the number of passages affording this sort of handle to misapprehension should have been so inconsiderable; and that, notwithstanding all the fastidious caution of the Fathers, on this subject, such a mass of explicit evidence should still be found in their writings;—evidence so abundant and convincing as, with any unbiassed mind, to place the truth of the Catholic doctrine, respecting the Eucharist, beyond all question.

It was in the third century, when the followers of Christ were most severely tried by the fires of persecution, that the discipline of secresy, with respect to this and the other mysteries, was most strictly observed. "A faithful concealment," says Tertullian, "is due to all mysteries from the very nature and constitution of them. How much more must it be due to *such mysteries as, if they were once discovered, could not escape immediate punishment from the hand of man.*" (Ad Nation. L. 1.) It may be conceived with what peculiar force such a motive to secresy would be likely to act upon minds naturally timid,—such as that of St. Cyprian, for instance, whose indisposition to martyrdom, however firmly he at last met it, when inevitable, was evinced on more than one occasion when he prudently withdrew himself from its grasp. We find, accordingly, in conformity with this timidity of character, that, among the observers of the Discipline of the Secret, he is allowed to have been one of the most circumspect and close.

It is, indeed, curious, not only as illustrative of the character of the individual, but as part of that kindred destiny which seems to have attended, throughout, the two Catholic dogmas of the Trinity and the Real Presence, that the same cautious St. Cyprian who, in his public letter to the Proconsul of Africa, thought it prudent to keep the Trinity entirely out of sight, should have been also the individual who, by his evasive language, concerning the Eucharist, has been the means of furnishing the opponents of a real, corporal

Presence with almost the only semblance of plausible authority by which they support their heresy*. Little did he think, good Saint, that a day would come, when this prudence, or timidity, would be made to pass for orthodoxy, and when,—sturdy a stickler as he was for the supremacy of the Roman See,—he should attain the eminence, such as it is, of being the prime Saint of Protestants!

It would be amusing,—were not so awful a point of faith the subject of such trifling, —to observe the self-complacent triumph with which a Protestant controvertist sits brooding over one of these intentionally unmeaning passages of the Fathers, hatching it into an argument. It matters not that the holy writer from whom the passage is extracted has, in

---

* Even St. Cyprian, however, could not help, on occasion, letting the true doctrine escape. Thus he says that, in the Eucharist, " we touch Christ's body and drink his blood;" and, in an Epistle to Pope Cornelius, speaking of the victims of persecution, he says, " How shall we teach them to shed their blood for Christ, if, before they go to battle, we do not give them *his* blood?"

a hundred others, pregnant both with meaning and with truth, borne testimony to the belief of his Church in that mighty miracle,—that fulfilment of a God's express promise which takes place under the veil of the Eucharist. It matters not:—the one convenient passage is alone brought forward again and again; the professional controvertist must still show himself in the lists, however " falsified *" his armour; and though *self*-deception is not always practicable in such cases, the great point is still gained of deceiving others.

The argument drawn from the occasional application of the words " type," " sign," " figure," &c. to the Eucharist, I have already disposed of; and a large proportion of the passages cited, as favourable to the Protestant side of the question, come under this predicament. One of the most triumphant pieces of evidence, however, (as they themselves consider it,) which the champions of the Reformed

* " His shield is falsified"—a meaning of the word which Dryden attempted to introduce, from the Italian.

Faith are in the habit of bringing forward to prove that Transubstantiation was not the belief of the early Church, is to be found in a passage or two from Theodoret and Gelasius (writers of the Fifth Century) in which it is asserted that the nature and substance of the sacramental elements remain after consecration. The extract from Theodoret I shall here transcribe, as well because it affords a curious insight into the operation of the Discipline of the Secret, as because it will show to what straits the opponents of the Catholic doctrine must be driven, when they can contrive to extract grounds for triumph from such testimony.

It is necessary to premise that the passage I am about to give is from a work written by Theodoret against the Eutychians (a sect of heretics who denied the human nature of Christ)*; and that, of the two fictitious persons

---

* It cannot be said correctly that Eutyches denied the humanity of Christ,—his belief being that, after the incarnation, there was no longer any distinction between the divine and human nature, but that the latter had been ab-

who discuss the question together, Orthodoxus represents the Catholic, and Eranistes the Eutychian. Having established, in a preceding Dialogue, the reality of Christ's presence in the Sacrament, the speakers thus proceed:—" *Eran.* I am happy you have mentioned the Divine Mysteries. Tell me, therefore, what do you call the gift that is offered before the Priest's invocation?—*Orth.* This must not be said openly; for some may be present who are not initiated.—*Eran.* Answer then in hidden terms.—*Orth.* We call it an aliment made of certain grains.—*Eran.* And how do you call the other symbol?— *Orth.* We give it a name that denotes a certain beverage.—*Eran.* And, after the con-

---

sorbed into the former, as a drop of honey, according to his illustration, would be swallowed up on falling into the sea. By the Council of Chalcedon which, in 451, condemned this heresy, the orthodox doctrine of the Trinity was at length fully established;—the union of the *two* distinct natures in Christ, and its correspondence with that of the *three* persons in the Godhead, being then definitely laid down.

secration, what are they called?—*Orth.* The body of Christ and the blood of Christ.—*Eran.* And you believe that you partake of the body and blood of Christ?—*Orth.* So I believe.—*Eran.* As the symbols then of the body and blood of Christ were different before the consecration of the Priest, and, after that consecration, become changed, and are something else, in the same manner we Eutychians say, the body of Christ after his ascension was changed into the divine essence.—*Orth.* Thou art taken in thy own snare; for, after the consecration, the mystical symbols lose not their proper nature; they remain both in the figure and appearance of their former substance, to be seen, and to be felt, as before; but they are understood to be what they have been made; this they are believed to be, and as such they are adored."

We have here (in a conference, be it remembered, supposed to have passed before the non-initiated) three no less important points acknowledged than,—first, a change into " something else " of the symbols after consecration *,—secondly, a Real Presence of the body and blood of Christ,—and, thirdly, adoration paid to the Sacrament, in consequence. The only doubt the passage admits of is, whether, contrary to the Catholic doctrine on the subject, Orthodoxus means to assert that the substance of the bread and wine remains after consecration; or whether, as the Catholic writers answer, the word " substance," as here used, means merely the external or sensible qualities of the elements, —those which, as Theodoret says, may be " seen and felt as before." The phrase "*former* substance," which seems to imply that a second substance has taken the place of the first, might certainly warrant the assumption that the whole passage was meant orthodoxly; but the fairest conclusion, perhaps, to come to (and the Catholic can well

---

* The same writer, in another place, asserts it to be Christ's " will that we should believe in a change, made by Grace" in the symbols :—εβουλκθη . . . . . . πιστευειν τη εκ της χαριτος γεγενημενη μεταβολη.

afford to be candid on this head,) is that Theodoret may have had some such vague notion, as Luther, afterwards, contrary to the sense of all Christian antiquity, adopted, of the presence of the substance of Christ's body and blood, in the sacrament, *together with* the substance of the bread and wine. On turning, indeed, to the volume of this Father's works, edited by Garnier, I find it to have been the opinion of that learned Jesuit —after an impartial inquiry into the exact belief of his author, respecting the *modus* of Christ's presence,—that Theodoret had, on the whole, a leaning to the Consubstantial heresy.

Such, taken at its very worst, is the full extent of that lapse from orthodoxy into which, at most, two Fathers, out of the whole sacred band of the five first centuries, can be said to have fallen on this subject,—the apparent deviations of others being, as I have shown, easily accounted for,—and such the quantum and quality of that evidence against the doctrine of the ancient Catholic Church which every successive champion of Protestantism brings forward, each triumphing in the discovery of the same worn out Fools' Paradise. The true view of such insulated instances of heterodoxy is to be found in the following remarks which the subject has drawn forth from the editor of that valuable compilation, " The Faith of Catholics:"—" Should it be conceded that there is ambiguity in these expressions, or that even the authors of them meant to convey a sense, in our estimation, heterodox, how light must their authority be, when balanced against the massive evidence of so many writers of their own age, and of the preceding centuries!—' Since the ancients,' says Erasmus, ' to whom the Church, not without reason, gives so much authority, are all agreed in the opinion, that the true substance of the body and blood of Jesus is in the Eucharist; since, in addition to all this has been added the constant authority of the Synods, and so perfect an agreement of the Christian world, let us also agree with them in this heavenly mystery, and let us receive, here below, the bread and the chalice of the Lord, under the veil of the species, until we eat and drink him without veil in the kingdom of God.'"

To this citation from Erasmus, I shall add another from a writer worthy to be named along with that great man, the pious and powerful Pascal, by whom the views of the Eucharist presented in the above sentences are thus more fully unfolded:—" The state of Christians, as Cardinal du Perron, in accordance with the opinions of the Fathers, remarks, holds a middle place between the state of the Blessed and that of the Jews. The Blessed possess Jesus Christ really, without figure and without veil. The Jews possessed of Christ only the figures and the veils,—such as were the Manna and the Paschal Lamb; and the Christians possess Jesus Christ in the Eucharist, veritably and really, but still covered with a veil. . . . . Thus is the Eucharist completely suited to the state of faith in which we are placed, since it contains Christ within it really, but still Christ veiled. Insomuch that this state would be destroyed, were Christ not really under the species of bread and wine, as the heretics pretend; and it would be also destroyed, did we receive him unveiled as they do in heaven ; seeing that this would be to confound our state, in the former case, with that of Judaism, in the latter, with that of Glory."

The reader who has thus far accompanied me from the beginning of my inquiries, and who knows the dogged resolution to turn Protestant with which I set out, will feel anxious, perhaps, to be informed whether, at the period where we are now arrived, any traces of my original resolve still lingered in my mind; or whether, with proofs clear as daylight, before my eyes, of the true holiness of my "first love," I had still lurking in my heart any desire of apostasy to another. Alas, so humiliating would be the confessions and explanations which an attempt to answer this inquiry must draw from me, that most willingly do I reserve them for some future opportunity; and, in the mean time, shall only say that it was not from any blindness to the light,—from any want of a deep conviction of the truths that had opened upon me, if, at the bottom of my heart, some worldly longings still lingered. There even *were* moments (such as I experienced on reading the passages just cited) when the unworthy "spirit of the world" died away within me,—when such a flood of religious feelings came over my heart as would not suffer any baser thoughts to live in their current, and when I was, in soul and mind, all Catholic, without a "shadow of turning." In this mood was it that, after closing the pages of the two great men I have just mentioned, I went to my pillow, pondering over the long list of illustrious sages,—the Erasmuses, Pascals, Fenelons, Leibnitzes, Sir Thomas Mores,—who have each, in turn, bowed, with implicit faith, before the miracle of the Eucharist, till, elevated above my own conscious nothingness by the contemplation of such men, I found myself, as I laid down my head, fervently saying, "Let my soul be with theirs!"

CHAPTER XVI.

Relaxation of the Discipline of the Secret, on the subject of the Trinity.—Doctrine of the Real Presence still concealed.—The Eucharists of the Heretics.—The Artoturites, Hydroparastatæ, &c.—St. Augustin a strict observer of the Secret.—Similar fate of Transubstantiation and the Trinity.

ABOUT the beginning of the fourth century, the Discipline of the Secret had been, on some important points, considerably relaxed; and though the Eucharist still continued to be guarded with some strictness, the doctrine of the Trinity was, by degrees, suffered to escape from behind the veil. The Edict of Toleration which was, at that period, issued by Constantine, gave to the Christians full security in the promulgation of their opinions; while the schism of Arius, by calling into question the divinity of the Saviour, not only rendered a declaration of the Church's doctrine on this subject necessary, but led naturally, from the sifting controversies to which it gave rise, to a more definite marking out of the frontiers of Trinitarian orthodoxy than had yet been attempted. Still it was but by slow and cautious degrees that the entire dogma, in its perfect form, as acknowledged now, was developed. I have before quoted a passage from a Father of this age where he says, " Of the Mysteries concerning the Father, Son, and Holy Spirit, we do not speak plainly before the Catechumens;" and, according to the learned Huet (himself a Catholic), " it is certain that the Catholics durst not plainly own the divinity of the Holy Spirit so late as the days of Basil."

In the mean time, the doctrine of the Real Presence,—following, for once, a fate different from that of its fellow mystery, the Trinity,—continued, as usual, to be whispered, in the inner shrines, to the neophyte, while, as Gregory of Nyssa informs us. the Eternal Sonship was become a topic of dispute among the lowest mechanics. Had any schism respecting the Eucharist taken place within the Church, the necessity of defending the doctrine would have led doubtless, as in the case of the Trinity, to the divulging of it. But no such schism had occurred. Those among the Gnostic sects who adopted the Eucharist, though they denied the real humanity of Christ's body, did not question its presence in the sacrament, while some of them even believed, with the orthodox, in a change of the elements, by the power of the Holy Spirit. " The *things*," says the heretic, Theodotus, " *are not what they appear to be*, or what they are apprehended to be; but by the power (of the Spirit) *are changed* into a spiritual power*."

One of these sects, indeed, proceeded so far, in rivalry of the Catholic Eucharist, as to contrive, by some mechanical process, to produce the appearance of blood flowing into the chalice †, after the words of consecration,—

---

* Ὁ ἄρτος ἁγιάζεται τῇ δυνάμει τοῦ πνεύματος, οὐ τὰ αὐτὰ ὄντα κατὰ τὸ φαινόμενον διὰ πληθὺν, ἀλλὰ δυνάμει εἰς δύναμιν πνευματικὴν μεταβέβληται.

† " Il (Marc) avoit deux vases, un plus grand et un plus petit; il mettoit le vin destiné à la célébration du sacrifice de la Messe dans le petit vase, et faisoit une prière: un instant après la liqueur bouillonnoit dans le grand vase, et

thereby outdoing, as they thought, the orthodox in, at least, the outward show of the miracle. In thus counterfeiting, by means of real liquid, that blood of which they, at the same time, *denied* the reality, these heretics were, of course, as absurd as knavish; but the testimony which their trick bears to the antiquity of the Catholic doctrine is not the less valuable. Were any additional proof, indeed, wanting of the prevalence, in those times, of a belief in the transubstantiation of the wine into blood, this effort of the Marcionite heretics to outbid, if I may so say, the orthodox altar in its marvels would abundantly furnish it.

There were also some other sects, besides the Gnostic, that adopted peculiar notions of their own respecting this sacrament. The

l'on y voyoit du sang au lieu du vin. Ce vase n'étoit apparemment que ce que l'on appelle communément la fontaine des nôces de Cana; c'est un vase dans lequel on verse de l'eau, l'eau versée fait monter du vin que l'on a mis auparavant dans ce vase et dont il se remplit."—*Mémoires pour servir à l'Histoire des Egaremens de l'Esprit Humain, &c. &c.*

Artoturites, for instance, a branch of the Montanists, offered bread and cheese in their religious rites. The Hydroparastatæ, from a regard to sobriety, used only water in the Eucharistic Sacrifice. Among the Ophites, who worshipped the serpent that tempted Eve, the sacrament consisted of a loaf, round which a serpent they kept always sacredly in a cage had been suffered to crawl and twine himself; and there was a sect of Manichæans who, holding bread to be one of the productions of the Evil Principle, kneaded up the paste of which they composed their Eucharist in a way too abominable to be mentioned.

These heresies, however, though on so vital a point of doctrine, yet, having been engendered out of the pale of the church[*], and being, all of them, with the exception of that of the Phantastics, limited and obscure, were not thought important enough to break the silence

---

[*] St. Cyprian, on being consulted respecting the nature of Novitian's errors, answers, " There is no need of a strict inquiry *what errors* he teaches, while he *teaches out of the Church.*"

of the Church respecting this mystery. The doctrine of the Real Presence, therefore, undisturbed by dissent and sacred from controversy, was left, partly through policy and partly through habit, enshrined in all its forms of mystery during the whole of the fourth century; and how well the secret was still guarded from the Catechumens as late as the time of St. Augustin may be seen from the following remarkable passage:—" Christ does not commit himself to Catechumens. Ask a Catechumen, Dost thou believe?—He answers, I do, and signs himself with the cross of Christ;—he is not ashamed of the cross of Christ, but bears it in his forehead. If we ask him, however, Dost thou eat the flesh and drink the blood of the Son of Man? he knows not what we mean, for Christ hath not committed himself to him. Catechumens do not know what Christians receive*."

---

* " Interrogemus eum, Manducas carnem Filii Hominis et bibis sanguinem? Nescit quid dicimus, quia Jesus non se credidit ei. Nesciunt Catechumeni quid accipiant Christiani."—*Tractat. in Joann.*

St. Augustin himself, from the peculiar circumstances of his position, was induced occasionally, on this subject, to adopt a reserve and ambiguity of language which are not to be found, in the same degree, in any of the writers of his period. Living, as he did, in Africa, where the population was still, for the greater part, Pagan, he deemed it prudent, evidently, to follow the ancient practice of the Church, and in the presence of all but the Faithful, to speak of this Mystery with caution. Hence is it that, though in none of the other Fathers are there to be found passages more strongly confirmatory of the ancient and Catholic faith*, on this point, he has, in some instances, employed language of whose vagueness and ambiguity the Sacramentarians have, as usual, taken advantage for the bolstering up of their desperate cause†. How barefaced,

---

* Alger, who defended the doctrine of Transubstantiation against Bérenger, refuted him chiefly, if not entirely, by passages out of St. Augustin.

† Even by Zuingle, however, it is not asserted that St. Augustin was against transubstantiation, but merely that he *would* have been so, could he have ventured to express

however, must be the assurance that would claim St. Augustin as a Protestant authority on this head, will appear by the following extracts from his writings:—" When, committing to us his body, he said, *This is my body*, Christ was held in his own hands. He bore that body in his hands."—*Enarrat.* 1. *in Psalm.* 33.—Again, in another Sermon on the same Psalm, he thus, in the mystic language of the Secret, expresses himself:—" How was he borne in his hands? Because, when *he gave his own body and blood*, he took into his hands *what the Faithful know* *; and he *bore*

his opinion freely. This he was forced, says Zuingle, in some measure, to conceal on account of the very general prevalence which the belief in a real fleshly Presence had, at that time, obtained.—*De ver. et fals. religione.* And here, we may be allowed to ask, how is this admission of Zuingle, with respect to the prevalence of such a belief in the time of St. Augustin, to be reconciled with that other favourite theory of the Protestants, which supposes the doctrine of Transubstantiation to have been first introduced by the monk, Paschasius, in the ninth century? But it is useless to ask such questions,—there being, in fact, no end to the inconsistencies and contrarieties of Protestants on this subject.

* " *Quod nôrunt fideles.*"—These words, or, as expressed

Himself in a certain manner, when he said, '*This is my body.*'"—In his Exposition of the 98th Psalm, he says, " Christ took upon him earth from the earth, because flesh is from the earth, and this flesh he took from the flesh of Mary : and because he here walked in this flesh, *even this same flesh he gave us to eat* for our salvation ;—but no one eateth this flesh without having *first adored* it ; and not only we do not sin by adoring, but we *even sin by not adoring it*."

It was my intention originally, as the reader possibly recollects, not to include the Fathers of the fifth century,—to which period Augustin more properly belongs,—within

---

in Greek, ισασιν οἱ μεμυημενοι, formed what may be called the watch-word of the Secret, and occur constantly in the Fathers. Thus St. Chrysostom, for instance,—in whose writings Casaubon remarked the recurrence of this phrase, at least, fifty times,—in speaking of the tongue (Comment. in Psalm. 143) says, " Reflect that this is the member with which we receive the tremendous sacrifice,—*the Faithful know what I speak of.*" Hardly less frequent is the occurrence of the same phrase in St. Augustin, who seldom ventures to intimate the Eucharist in any other way than by the words " Quod nôrunt Fideles."

the range of these inquiries; but an exception, in favour of so important an authority, will without difficulty be admitted. The brief history, too, which I have attempted to give of the Eucharist, through the " aurea secula" of the Church, would have been left imperfect without the testimony which the passage, just cited, furnishes; a testimony valuable, as proving the general belief of a Real Presence in this Sacrament, by that best practical evidence, the adoration paid to it,—the belief and the practice implying reciprocally each other.

I have already intimated that most of the writers contemporary with, or just preceding St. Augustin, have, as compared with him, spoken frankly on the subject of the Eucharist. It was not possible, indeed, that such a developement as, about this period, took place of a doctrine hitherto so inshrined in obscurity as was the Trinity, should not encourage by degrees a boldness of language and thought which would show itself in the assertion of the other great mysteries. Accordingly we find,—not only in the catechetical discourses of this time, but even in writings more intended for the public eye,—a far more explicit testimony to the doctrine of the Real Presence and of the change of substance than had been ventured on since the days of St. Justin and St. Irenæus. It is worthy of remark, too,—as adding another illustration to the many I have already noticed of the similar fate that has, in most instances, attended these twin mysteries, Transubstantiation and the Trinity, —that the same eminent men who, in the fourth century, carried the latter dogma to that high region of orthodoxy where it stands fixed at present, were also those who asserted most boldly the entire Catholic doctrine respecting the Eucharist;—the same Gregory of Nyssa who held that " the bread sanctified by the Word of God was transmuted into the body of the Word of God" having been also the strenuous maintainer of the doctrine, " that there was a whole Son in a whole Father, and a whole Father in a whole Son;" and the same Gregory of Nazianzum who desired his hearers " not to stagger in their souls, but, without shame or doubting, to eat the body and drink the blood," having likewise told them that " whoever maintains that any of the Three Persons is inferior to the others overturns the whole Trinity."

CHAPTER XVII.

Fathers of the Fourth Century.—Proofs of their doctrine respecting the Eucharist.—Ancient Liturgies.

HAVING now laid before my reader the whole process of thought and inquiry by which that phantom of Protestantism which had, as I fancied, beckoned to me out of the pages of St. Clement and St. Cyprian was again explained away into "thin air," I shall now select a few of the innumerable passages that abound throughout the writings of the fourth century, bearing testimony incontrovertible to the true nature both of the Blessed Eucharist itself, and of all the rites and doctrines connected with that mystery,—the altar, the oblation, the unbloody sacrifice, the real presence of the victim, the change of substance, and, as the natural consequence of all, the adoration.

St. James of Nisibis*.—" Our Lord gave his body with his own hands, for food; and his blood for drink, before he was crucified †."
—*Serm.* 14.

" Abstain from all uncleanness, and then

---

* A distinguished Bishop who assisted at the Council of Nice, in 325, and was, as Cave describes him, " doctrinæ orthodoxæ vindex primarius." This Father, indeed, deserves to be included among those mentioned in the preceding Chapter as having maintained an equally high tone of orthodoxy in both the great Christian mysteries, the Trinity and the Real Presence.

† " Christ offered himself, as a Priest, before his crucifixion."—See *Johnson's Unbloody Sacrifice.*—This learned Protestant, who, like Grabe, Chillingworth, and other ornaments of the same Church, was sufficiently open to the light of truth to adhere to the ancient Catholic doctrine of the Eucharistic Sacrifice, thus expresses himself on the subject in another part of his work:—" I suppose all Protestants will allow that Christ's sacrifice was intended for the expiation of sin; and, if so, they cannot think it strange that it was offered before it was slain, and that by the Priest himself;—for it is clear this was the method prescribed by Moses of old."—And, again, " We may safely conclude that he did then offer himself, while alive; especially since sacrifices of expiation and consecration were, of old, thus offered by the Priest before they were slain."

receive the body and blood of Christ. Cautiously guard your *mouth, through which the Lord has entered,* and be it no longer a passage to words of uncleanness."—*Serm.* 3.

St. Ephrem of Edessa.—" Consider, my beloved, with what fear those stand before the throne, who wait on a mortal King. *How much more does it behove us to appear before the heavenly King with fear and trembling, and with awful gravity?* Hence it becomes us not boldly to look on the mysteries, that lie before us, of the body and blood of our Lord."—*Parœn.* 19. " *The eye of faith manifestly beholds the Lord, eating his body and drinking his blood, and indulges no curious inquiry* *. You believe that Christ, the Son

---

* The counsel here given, not to pry curiously into the mysteries of the Faith, is inculcated frequently in the writings of the Fathers. Thus St. Ambrose says—" Manum ori admove;—scrutari non licet superna mysteria." *(De Abrah. Patr.)* St. Cyril of Alexandria lays it down, too, with equal solemnity that all curiosity is to be refrained from in matters of faith:—το πιστει παραδεκτον απολυπραγμονητον ειναι χρη.—Had the Fathers themselves somewhat more attended to this caution, much of the trifling speculation into which they have entered, touching

of God, for you was born in the flesh. Then why do you search into what is inscrutable? Doing this, you prove your curiosity, not your faith. *Believe, then, and with a firm faith receive the body and blood of our Lord."*—De Nat. Dei.

St. Cyril of Jerusalem*.—" The bread and

---

the manner in which Christ's body unites itself with the bodies of those who receive it, would have been, with advantage, avoided. St. Cyril of Alexandria compares the union which thus takes place to that of lead with silver; while another Father sees in it a resemblance to the mixing up of leaven with paste. A third says it is like the melting of one piece of wax into another; while, by some, an illustration of the mystery is sought for, in the manner in which medicine passes into the entrails.

Such attempts to solve what is inexplicable but afford triumph to the infidel and the heretic; and, accordingly, in the controversy which gave rise to the celebrated work "De la Perpétuité de la Foi," we find the Reformed Ministers profanely reproaching the Catholics with believing that the body of Christ is received " comme on mange des pilules."

* The Discourses of St. Cyril, from which these extracts are taken, were addressed to those Christians who were newly baptized, and who had therefore but recently been admitted to the Mysteries.

The learned and Protestant author of a very useful

wine which before the invocation of the Adorable Trinity were nothing but bread and wine, *become, after this invocation, the body and blood of Christ.*"—Catech. Mystag. 1. "The *Eucharistic bread*, after the invocation of the Holy Spirit, *is no longer common bread, but the body of Christ.*"—Catech. 3. "As then Christ, speaking of the bread, declared, and said 'This is my body,' who shall dare to doubt it? And as, speaking of the wine, he positively assured us, and said 'This is my blood,' who shall doubt it and say that it is not

work, lately published (Clarke's *Succession of Ecclesiastical Literature*) expresses strong doubts as to the authenticity of these Discourses of Cyril, but omits to assign any reasons for his doubts. We have against him, indeed, high Protestant authorities. "To question," says Cave, "whether these Discourses be Cyril's (as some have done) is foolish and trifling; when they are not only quoted by Damascen, but expressly mentioned by St. Jerom, and cited by Theodoret, the one contemporary with him, the others flourishing but a few years after him."

The distinguished theologian, Bishop Bull, contends also most strenuously against those who would contest the authenticity of these Catecheses, and the opinions of Vossius, Whitaker, and other learned Protestants may be cited on the same side.

his blood?"—*Catech. Myst.* 4. "Jesus Christ, in Cana of Galilee, *once changed water into wine by his will only;* and shall we think him less worthy of credit, *when he changes wine into blood?*"—Ibid. "Wherefore I conjure you, my brethren, not to consider them any more as common bread and wine, since they are the body and blood of Jesus Christ according to his words; and, although your sense might suggest that to you, let faith confirm you. *Judge not of the thing by your taste, but by faith assure yourself, without the least doubt, that you are honoured with the blood and body of Christ:—this knowing, and of this being assured, that what appears to be bread is not bread, though it be taken for the bread by the taste, but is the body of Christ; and that which appears to be wine, is not the wine, though the taste will have it so, but the blood of Christ.*"—Ibid*.

* St. Cyril of Alexandria, who lived in the succeeding century, is, if any thing, still more express and emphatic in asserting a real, corporal Presence than his namesake of Jerusalem. Thus, in his Homily on the Mystic Sup-

St. Basil.—" About the things that God has spoken there should be no hesitation nor doubt, but a *firm persuasion that all is true and possible, though Nature be against it**. Herein lies the struggle of faith."—*Regula* viii. *Moral.* " The words of the Lord, ' This is my body, which shall be delivered for

per, he pronounces Christ to be "both Priest and Victim, him that offers and that is offered." In his Commentary on St. John, too, we find the following passages:—" And what is the meaning and the efficacy of this Mystic Eucharist? is it not that Christ may *corporally dwell in us by the participation and communion of his holy flesh?*"— " By the mediation of Christ, therefore, we enter into a union with God the Father, receiving him within us, *corporally* and *spiritually*, who by nature truly is the Son, and consubstantial with him."

Another Holy Father, Isidore of Pelusium, who lived at the commencement of the same age and was one of the Disciples of St. Chrysostom, thus, in writing against Macedonius who denied the Divinity of the Holy Ghost, brings, as a proof of the Spirit's Divine nature, the miracle of Transubstantiation:—" Since it is he who, on the mysterious table, *produces from common bread the very body of Jesus Christ incarnate.*"—Ep. ad Marathon. Monach.

* Παν ρημα Θεου αληθες ειναι και δυνατον, καν η φυσις μαχηται.

you,' create a firm conviction."—*Ibid. in Reg. brev.*

St. Gregory of Nyssa.—" What is this medicine? *No other than that body which was shown to be more powerful than death, and was the beginning of our life; and which could not otherwise enter into our bodies than by eating and drinking.* Now, we must consider, how it can be, that one body, which so constantly, through the whole world, is distributed to so many thousands of the faithful, can be whole in each receiver, and itself remain whole*. This bread, as the Apostle says, is sanctified by the Word of God and prayer,—not that, as food, it passes into the body, but that it is *instantly changed into the body of Christ,* agreeably to what he said, ' This is my body†.' "—*Orat. Catech.*

---

* Bonaventura illustrates this miracle by the example of a mirror, which, when broken, repeats, in each several fragment, the same entire image which it had reflected, when whole.

† " The thirty-seventh Chapter (of Gregory of Nyssa's Great Catechetical Discourse) treats of the Eucharist, where he fully and clearly avows the doctrine of the Real

St. Gregory of Nazianzum.—" The law puts a staff in your hand, that you may not stagger in your souls, when you hear of the blood, passion and death of God: but rather *without shame and doubting, eat the body and drink the blood,* if you sigh after life, never doubting of what you hear concerning his flesh, nor scandalized at his passion."—*Orat.* 42.

St. Ambrose.—" *Perhaps you will say, why do you tell me that I receive the body of Christ, when I see quite another thing?* We have this point, therefore, to prove. How many examples do we produce to show you that *this is not what nature made it, but what the benediction has consecrated it;* and that the benediction is of greater force than nature, *because, by the benediction, nature itself is changed.* Moses cast his rod on the ground, and it

---

Presence—Καλως ουν και νυν τον τω λογω του Θεου αγιαζομενον αρτον εις σωμα του Θεου Λογου μεταποιεισθαι πιστευομαι."— *Clarke's Succession, &c.* It is, in like manner, acknowledged by the learned Protestant, Dr. Grabe, that Gregory of Nyssa and Cyril of Jerusalem both assert, in their writings, that the substance of bread in the Eucharist is transferred into the flesh of Christ which he took of the Virgin.

became a serpent; he caught hold of the serpent's tail, and it recovered the nature of a rod. . . . . Thou hast read of the Creation of the world: *if Christ, by his word, was able to make something out of nothing, shall he not be thought able to change one thing into another* ?*"—De Mysteriis.

Of this Discourse of St. Ambrose, the writer, referred to in the preceding note, says—" Had a work been *now* written on the Roman Catholic practice and doctrine of Baptism and *the Lord's Supper,* it *could not more fully assert the Papal creed on these points* than this Discourse." *(Clarke's Succession of Sacred Literature.)* After such admissions as this,—and no Protestant, with candour and knowledge, will gainsay its truth,—what becomes, I again ask, of the old wives' tale, still harped upon occasionally by a few worn-out controversialists, which would represent Transubstantiation as an *invention* of the *ninth* century?

In the Treatise *d Sacramentis,* attributed to St. Ambrose, we find equally strong and clear proofs of this Father's belief in Transubstantiation. As, for instance, " Though they may seem to be the figure of the bread and wine, yet, after the consecration, they must be believed to be the flesh and blood and nothing else." In noticing the doubts that have been raised as to the authenticity of this particular Treatise, Mr. Clarke observes, " The arguments seem strong against it; but, however it may be, it is clear, from the ascertained productions of

St. Jerom.—" Moses gave us not the true bread, but our Lord Jesus did. *He invites us to the feast, and is himself our meat: he eats with us, and we eat him.*"—Ep. 150, ad Hedib.

St. Gaudentius of Brescia.—" In the shadows and figures of the ancient Pasch, not one lamb, but many were slain, for each house had its sacrifice, because one victim could not suffice for all the people; and also because the mystery was a mere figure, and not the reality of the passion of the Lord. For the figure of a thing is not the reality, but only the image and representation of the thing signified. But now, when the figure has ceased, the one that died for all, immolated in the mystery of bread and wine, gives life through all the churches*, and, being

---

this author, that the doctrines contained in it are in accordance with his opinions; and the Real Presence, and the forms and ceremonies, &c. of Baptism, are just such as St. Ambrose would have delivered."

* Such passages as this, which abound in the writers of the fourth age, attributing a life-giving effect to the participation of the Eucharist, prove most clearly that the

consecrated, sanctifies those who consecrate. . . . . He who is the Creator and Lord of all natures, who produces bread from the earth, *of the bread makes his own proper body* (for he is able, and he promised to do it) and who of water made wine, and of wine his blood."—*Tract.* 11, *de Pasch.*

St. John Chrysostom.—" Let us believe God in every thing, and not gainsay him, *although what is said may seem contrary to our reason and our sight**. Let his word overpower both. *Thus let us do in mysteries, not looking only on the things that lie before us, but holding fast his words; for his word*

---

sixth chapter of St. John was understood by them as referring to that Sacrament. In this sense, Julius Firmicus, a writer of the fourth age, calls the Eucharistic chalice " poculum immortale," and adds that it bestows upon the dying the gift of eternal life. " And what do they hold (says St. Augustin) who call the Sacrament of the Lord's Table, Life, but that which was said, ' I am the Bread of Life, and except ye eat of me, ye shall have no life in you?'"

* The same Father defines the signification of a Mystery to be, " when we see one thing but believe it to be another"—ἑτερα ὁρωμεν, ἑτερα πιστευομεν.

cannot deceive; but our sense is very easily deceived. Since then his word says, 'This is my body,' let us assent and believe, and view it with the eyes of our understanding."—*Homil. 82, in Matt.* "As many as partake of this body, as many as taste of this blood, *think ye it nothing different from that which sits above, and is adored by angels."*—Homil. 3, in c. 1, ad Ephes. "Wonderful!—the table is spread with mysteries, the Lamb of God is slain for thee, and the spiritual blood flows from the sacred table. The spiritual fire comes down from heaven; the blood in the chalice is drawn from the spotless side for thy purification. *Thinkest thou that thou seest bread? that thou seest wine? that these things pass off as other foods do? Far be it from thee to think so. But, as wax brought near to the fire loses its former substance which no longer remains; so do thou thus conclude, that the mysteries* (the bread and wine) *are consumed by the substance of the Body.*"—Hom. 9, de Pœnit. "But are there many Christs, as the offering is made in many places? By no means: it is the same Christ every where; here entire, and there entire, one body. As then, though offered in many places, there is one body, and not many bodies; so is there one sacrifice."— *Hom.* 17, *in c.* 9, *ad Hebr.*

St. Maruthas.—" As often as we approach and receive on our hands the body and blood, we believe that we embrace his body, and become, as it is written, flesh of his flesh and bone of his bones. *For Christ did not call it the figure or species of his body, but he said, ' this truly is my body and this is my blood.'"* —Com. in Mat.

In addition to the decisive testimony of all the Fathers on this subject, there is yet another body of evidence, still more ancient and precious, to be found in those Liturgies of the early Churches, Greek, Latin, Arabic, Syriac, &c. which, like the Apostles' Creed, and for similar reasons, were handed down unwritten*, and preserved, in the memories of

---

* The Apostles' Creed is supposed to have been one of the Signs of the Secret, by which the Initiated, or bap-

the Faithful, from age to age. It was not till Christianity had found a refuge under the roofs of Kings that these depositories of her sacred rites, prayers and dogmas, were published to the world; and, whatever interpolations they may have, some of them, suffered in their progress, it is not doubted, among the learned, that, in those parts where they are found all to agree, they may be depended upon as authentic monuments of the apostolic times*. Their entire agreement, therefore, in the sense of those prayers which were used in consecrating the elements of the Eucharist †, is a proof more

---

tized, knew each other, and to have thence derived the designation of *Symbol*.—See *Hist. of Apostles' Creed.*

* It can hardly be doubted (says Archbishop Wake) " but that those prayers in which the Liturgies all agree, in sense, at least, if not in words, were first prescribed, in the same or like terms, by those Apostles and Evangelists" whose names they bear.—*Apostolic Fathers.*

† " I add to what has been already observed the consent of all the Christian Churches in the world, however distant from each other, in the holy Eucharist, or Sacrament of the Lord's Supper; which consent is indeed wonderful. All the ancient Liturgies agree in this form of prayer, almost in the same words, but fully and exactly

remarkable, perhaps, than any other that has been adduced, of the apostolical date of the Catholic doctrine on that subject. An extract or two from some of the most ancient of these Liturgies shall conclude this long Chapter.

Liturgy of Jerusalem (called also, the *Liturgy of St. James*).—" Have mercy on us, O God! the Father Almighty, and send thy Holy Spirit the Lord and giver of life, equal in dominion to thee and to thy son— who descended in the likeness of a dove on our Lord Jesus Christ—who descended on the holy Apostles in the likeness of tongues of fire—*that coming he may make this bread the life-giving body*, the saving body, the heavenly body, the body giving health to souls and bodies, the body of our Lord, God and Saviour, Jesus, for the remission of sins and eternal life to those who receive it.—

in the same sense, order and method; which whoever attentively considers must be convinced that this order of prayer was delivered to the several churches in the very first plantation and settlement of them."—*Bishop Bull, Sermons on Common Prayer.*

Amen. . . . . Wherefore we offer to thee, O Lord, *this tremendous and unbloody sacrifice* for thy holy places which thou hast enlightened by the manifestation of Christ, thy son," &c. &c.

Liturgy of Alexandria (called also, the *Liturgy of St. Mark*).—" Send down upon us, and upon this bread, and this chalice, thy Holy Spirit, that he may sanctify and consecrate them, as God Almighty, and *make the bread indeed the body and the chalice the blood** of the New Testament of* the very Lord, and God, and Saviour, and our sovereign King, Jesus Christ," &c. &c.

Roman Liturgy (called also, the *Liturgy of St. Peter*).—" We beseech thee, O God, to cause that this oblation may be, in all

---

* " I find," says the Protestant Grotius, " in *all the Liturgies*, Greek, Latin, Arabic, Syriac and others, prayers to God that he would consecrate, by his Holy Spirit, the gifts offered, and *make them the body and blood* of his Son. I was right, therefore, in saying that a custom so ancient and universal that it must be considered to have come down from the primitive times, ought not to have been changed."—*Votum pro Pace*.

things, blessed, admitted, ratified, reasonable and acceptable; that *it may become for us the body and blood of thy beloved Son, our Lord Jesus Christ.*" At the Communion, bowing down in sentiments of profound *adoration* and humility, and addressing himself to Jesus Christ then present in his hand, he says thrice, " Lord, I am not worthy that thou shouldst enter under my roof; but say only the word and my soul shall be healed."

Liturgy of Constantinople.—" Bless, O Lord, the holy bread—*make, indeed, this bread the precious body of thy Christ.* Bless, O Lord, the holy chalice; and what is in this chalice, the precious blood of thy Christ—*changing by the Holy Spirit.*" . . . . Then, dividing the holy bread into four parts, the Priest says, " 'The Lamb of God is broken and divided,—the Son of the Father, he is broken, but not diminished; he is always eaten, but is not consumed; but he sanctifies those who are made partakers."

CHAPTER XVIII.

Visit to T———d-street Chapel.—Antiquity of the observances of the Mass.—Lights, Incense, Holy Water, &c.—Craw-thumpers.—St. Augustin a Craw-thumper.—Imitations of Paganism in the early Church.

It was, I recollect, late on a Saturday night, when my task of selecting the extracts given in the preceding chapter was completed; and so strong, I confess, was the yearning with which I found myself drawn back to old Mother Church by so many irresistible proofs of her pure Christian descent, that, on the following morning, for the first time since I had ceased to be a boy, I went to attend the celebration of mass in T———d-street Chapel. It was as a sort of peace-offering to the manes of my venerable old confessor, Father O'———, that I thus chose the chapel to which he had belonged, as the scene of the Prodigal's Return, and,—like those mariners of old who used to hang up their votive tablets in the temple, after escaping from shipwreck,—went to offer up a short prayer on my arrival, safe and sound, from this long and adventurous cruise after that phantom-ship, primitive Protestantism.

But, though returning thus to the mansion of her who had nursed me, *was* I, indeed, " worthy to be called her son ?"—Though my reason had been so fully, so abundantly convinced, was that worst source of error, " the blindness of the heart," yet removed ? My readers themselves will know but too well how to answer this question, when I confess, that so ashamed did I feel even of the slight hankering after my former faith which this visit to the chapel betrayed, that I took care to place myself where I should be least likely to meet with persons who knew me; and even there cowered in my corner so as to be, as much as possible, concealed.

Though it is evident, from all this, that my *feeling* of religion had gained but little by my late course of sacred studies, my stock of *knowledge* on the subject could not be otherwise than considerably increased. Far different, indeed, were the thoughts with which I now witnessed the ceremonies of that altar from those which they had awakened in me in my boyish days. I had then blindly revered all its forms, without knowing what they meant; I was now book-learned in their history and their import, but—where was the feeling? It was, I blush to own, far more with the zeal of an antiquary than of a Catholic, or Christian, that, as I now peeped from my corner, I took pleasure in tracing, through every part of the service, some doctrine or observance of the primitive times, and admiring the watchful fidelity with which Tradition had handed down every little ceremony connected with that dawn of our faith.

In the use of lights and incense,—a practice sneered at by the Protestant, as pagan,— I but read the touching story of the early Church, when her children, hunted by the persecutor, held their religious meetings either at night, or in subterranean places*, whose

---

* Ciampini, in his curious work on the remains of ancient buildings and Mosaics, denies that the primitive

gloom, of course, rendered the light of tapers* necessary, and where the fumes of the censer, besides being familiar to the people among whom Christianity first sprung, were resorted to as a means of dissipating unwholesome odours. In sprinkling the Holy Water on my forehead, I called to mind the far period, —as early as the beginning of the second century,—when salt began to be mixed with the blessed water, in memory of Christ's death†; or, as others will have it, as a mystic type of the hypostatic union of the two natures in the Redeemer.

At that period of the Mass when the mysterious Sacrifice begins, I found myself reminded

---

Christians performed their worship in crypts, and asserts that their meetings were held in houses built over, or near, the cemeteries. This laborious antiquary numbers up a list of no less than eighty churches built by the Christians from the year 33 to 275.

* Thus we are told, in some notes on Eusebius *(De Die Dominico),* " Quod Christiani mane quondam congregati, Synaxes suas ad lumina accensa celebrarint, quæ deinceps, etiam interdiu retenta sunt."

† According to Tertullian, the sprinkling of the Holy Water was " in memoriam dedicationis Christi."

of the form of words, " Foris Catechumeni," in which invariably, as long as the Discipline of the Secret continued to be observed, the Catechumens, or unbaptized, were dismissed from Church, before those Mysteries, which none but the initiated were allowed to witness, commenced. By the words " Per quem hæc omnia, Domine*," my thoughts were recalled to the simplicity of the first ages, when the young fruits of the season used to be laid on the altar, and receive, in these words, the blessing of the Priest, before the Communion. Again, when I heard the Priest say " Lift up your hearts," and the people respond to him " We have lifted them up to the Lord," could I help remembering with reverence that in the very same phrases did St. Cyprian and his flock commune before their God[†], no less than fifteen hundred years since,—that is,

---

* By Calvin, Basnage, &c. an attempt has been made to turn this formula of the Ancient Mass into an argument against the doctrine of the Real Presence,—but the explanation given above is a sufficient answer to their cavils.

† *De Orat. Domin.*—St. Cyril of Jerusalem also makes mention of this formula, *Catech. Myst.* 5.

twelve whole centuries before any of those Protestants, by whom the Mass was abolished, existed!

But there occurred to me yet another proof of the high antiquity of the religious observances of the Catholics, which struck me the more forcibly inasmuch as it related to one of their most ridiculed practices, that of beating the breast with the clenched hand, at the Confiteor, and other parts of the service;— a practice which, in Ireland, has drawn down on the Papists the well-bred appellation of *craw-thumpers.* When I looked round, however, upon the humble Christians, thus nicknamed, and remembered that St. Augustin himself, the pious and learned St. Augustin, was also a *craw-thumper*, I felt that to err with him was, at least, erring in good company, and proceeded to join the " tundentes pectora" (as the Saint describes them*) with all my might.

The charge brought against the Catholics

---

* " Si non habemus peccata, et tundentes pectora, dicimus ' Dimitte nobis peccata nostra,' &c. &c."—*Serm* 35.

of being copyists of the Pagans is one regularly renewed by every tour-writing parson who returns, horror-struck with images, &c. from Rome and Naples. So far from denying, however, their adoption of some Pagan customs, the early Christians would have avowed and justified such a policy, as calculated to soften down that appearance of novelty in their faith which formed one of the most startling obstacles to its reception with the Heathen, and thus to enable them, by borrowing some of the forms of error, to win over their hearers to the substance of truth*.

The numerous vestiges, indeed, of Paganism, which partly from this policy, partly from the force of habit and imitation, were still retained in the ritual, language, and ceremonies of the early Church, would take far more space than my present limits can afford to

---

* The advantage of such a mode of proceeding is put acutely in the following words of Bede:—" Pertinaci Paganismo mutatione subventum est, quum rei in totum sublatio potiùs irritâsset."

enumerate them. Not to dwell on such instances as the adoption of the words "Mystery" and "Sacrament*" from the religious language of the Romans and Greeks,—the form of dismissal addressed to the Catechumens, at the commencement of the Sacrifice, " Depart, ye who are not initiated," in which we recognize the " Procul este, profani," of the Pagan mysteries,—the confession of sins, and abstinence from particular foods required by both religions of the candidates for initiation†, and the different stages or ranks through which they were, in each, gradually

---

* By Doctor Waterland the application of the word "Sacrament" to the Eucharist is traced to so early a date as that of the letter of Pliny respecting the Christians, in which he says, " Seque Sacramento non in scelus aliquod obstringere, sed ne furta, &c." But it is evident that Pliny here employs the word, in the Roman sense, as meaning an Oath; nor is there, I believe, any recorded instance of its application to the Eucharist before the time of Tertullian.

† After confessing their sins, the Heathen candidates were asked, " Have you eaten of the lawful food, and abstained from the unlawful?"—το σιτου και το μη σιτου δι εγευσω;

promoted*,—the special selection by the Christians of those days, for the Festivals of their Church, which had been before dedicated to some superstitious solemnity by the Pagans†,—not to dwell upon these and many other such striking points of resemblance, we can trace, even in the Liturgic service of the early Church, both the forms and language of the Pagan worship.

Thus that species of Psalmody, called Antiphony, first introduced into the Church by St. Ignatius, wherein the anthem was sung alternately by two choirs, was the mode of singing, according to Casaubon, that had been practised in the temples of the Gentiles;

---

* The last and highest stage of initiation was by the Heathen Mystagogues called Teletes, or the Consummation; and in the same manner, the admission of the Christian neophyte to communion is styled frequently by the Fathers ελθεῖν επι το τελειον.

† " Our Lord God," says Theodoret, " hath brought his dead (viz. the Martyrs) into the room and place of your Gods whom he hath sent about their business, and hath given their honour to his Martyrs. For, instead of the feasts of Jupiter and Bacchus are now celebrated the festivals of Peter and Paul," &c.

and the responses of the people to the Priests found a precedent in some of the ancient Bacchic rites:—" Praise God," said the Daduchus, or High Priest, and the people answered, " Oh son of Semele, bestower of wealth." The very words, indeed, *Kyrie Eleison*, " Lord have mercy on us," which have kept their place in all Litanies to the present day, were, as appears from Arrian (who wrote in the second century), the ordinary form of prayer to the Deity among the Pagans. " We pray to God (says Arrian, himself a Pagan) in the words *Kyrie Eleison**."

So far from denying, I repeat it, the source from which these forms have been derived, the Catholics are themselves among the first to avow it†; well knowing, however the Protestant may wish to blink such a conclusion, that these occasional resemblances to the

---

* Τον Θιον ιπικαλουμινοι διομιθα αυτου, Κυριι ιλιησον.—*Dissertat. Epictet.*

† The learned Brisson (one of the victims of the League) says expressly of the words Kyrie Eleison, in his work on the Forms of the Catholic Church, " Fontem hujus precationis esse à Paganorum consuetudine."

forms of Paganism, in the ceremonies of their Church, form one of the countless proofs she can give of the high antiquity of her descent,—even the outward formulary of her devotions being thus traceable to that bright dawn of Christianity, when truth gained upon error gradually, like light upon darkness; and when, if any such lingering mists remained from the night, they were but to be made subservient to the glory of the day.

CHAPTER XIX.

Ruminations.— Unity of the Catholic Church.— History of St. Peter's Chair.— Means of preserving Unity.— Irenæus.— Hilary.— Indefectibility of the one Church.

Surely, thought I, as, ruminating, I sauntered homewards from the chapel,—were there even no other evidence in favour of the authenticity of her claims, this adherence, on the part of the Catholic Church, through all changes of time and circumstance, to every, even the minutest point of discipline or worship on which the seal of her primitive teachers was set, would be, of itself, a sufficient assurance, without any further testimony, that she had kept equally scrupulous watch over the great doctrines bequeathed to her, and handed them down, even unto our own times, as they were " delivered by the Saints."

Though nothing less, of course, than the superintendence of a Divine Providence can be held sufficient to account for this great standing miracle of a Church upholding itself through the lapse of eighteen centuries, unchanged and, as it would appear, unchangeable,—it may yet be permitted to inquire how far, as a subordinate instrument, human policy may have had its share in producing this result; and there can be no doubt that the zealous watchfulness with which the pastors of the Catholic Church have ever acted upon, themselves, and prescribed urgently to their flocks the precept of St. Paul, " Be ye of one mind," has been, of all the human means employed to keep the strong fabric of their Faith unbroken, the most sagacious and powerful.

What importance they attached to Unity, and how great was their horror of schism, appears from the earnest language of all the Fathers on the subject. " Unity cannot be severed," says St. Cyprian, " nor the one body by laceration be divided. Whatever is separated from the stock, cannot live, cannot breathe apart: it loses the substance of life."—*De Unitat. Eccles.*
" The ancient Catholic Church alone (says St.

Clement of Alexandria) is one in essence, in opinion, in origin, and in excellence, one in faith."—*Strom. l.* 7. In a still more Popish spirit, St. Optatus (a bishop of Milevis in the fourth century) thus writes:—" You cannot deny that St. Peter, *the chief of the Apostles*, established an Episcopal Chair at Rome. *This Chair was one, that all might preserve Unity by the union which they had with it: so that, whoever set up a chair against it should be a schismatic and an offender.*"—De Schism. Donat.

The history, indeed, of this "one Chair" presents, in itself, such a phenomenon and marvel as no other form of human power, in any age of the world, has paralleled. Through a course of eighteen centuries, amidst the constant flux and reflux of the destinies of nations, while every other part of Europe has seen its institutions, time after time, broken up and reconstructed, while new races of kings have, like pageants, come and disappeared, and England herself has passed successively under the sway of five different nations, the Apostolic See, the Chair of St. Peter, has alone defied the vicissitudes of time,—has remained as "a city seated on a mountain," a rallying point for the church of God throughout all time, and counting an unbroken succession of Pontiffs* from its first occupant, St. Peter, down to the present hour.

To return, however, to the more directly human means by which the stability of the Catholic Church has been thus wonderfully preserved,—we have seen that to the maintenance of entire and changeless unity among her children, all the energies of her most enlightened pastors have, in all times, been directed; and such a system of union being, in fact, indispensable both to the peace and durability of their Church, it is of importance to inquire by what means they so well succeeded in effecting it. Was it by throwing

---

* In speaking of the first links of this chain,—from St. Peter down to Eleutherius, the 12th Bishop of Rome,—Irenæus says, "In this very order and succession has the *Tradition which is in the Church*, and the preaching of the truth, *come to us from the Apostles.*"

open the Scriptures to the multitude? Was it by leaving, like modern Reformers, the right of judgment unfettered, and allowing every man to interpret the Sacred Volume as he fancied? Far from it;—they were as little Protestant on this point as on all others. They asked, with St. Paul, "Are all Prophets? are all Teachers?" They knew, with St. Peter, that there are, in the Scriptures, "things hard to be understood, which the unlearned and unstable wrest to their own destruction." They saw the consequences of the first steps of dissent in the random course of all the heretics of their day; and the language employed by them in speaking of these vagrant sectaries was but an anticipation of what the Catholics of after-times have had to apply to Protestants. Thus St. Irenæus, who lived, if I may so say, in the very sunset of the apostolical age, and had its light fresh around him, after remarking the uncountable varieties of doctrine into which heresy had even then branched, adds :—" When, therefore, they shall be agreed among themselves on what they draw from the Scriptures, it will be our time to refute them. Meanwhile, thinking wrongfully, and not agreeing in the meaning of the same words, they convict themselves. But we, having one true and only God for our master, and making his words the rule of truth, always speak alike of the same things."—*Adv. Hær. l.* 4.*

Two centuries later we find the great Trinitarian, St. Hilary, describing the Arian creed-mongers of his own time in terms no less appropriately applicable to the Luthers, Zwingles, and Calvins of the Reformation, and to all those *succession* crops of Creeds

---

* In the same spirit is another remarkable passage of the same Father:—" Paul said, ' We speak wisdom among the Perfect, but not the wisdom of this world.' Every one of these men (the heretics) affirms that this wisdom is in himself; that he findeth it of himself,— namely, the fiction which he hath invented. So that, according to them, the truth is said to be sometimes in Valentinus, sometimes in Marcion, sometimes in Cerinthus, and, after that, in Basilides. *When again we appeal to that tradition,* which is delivered from the Apostles, and *which is preserved in the Church by a succession of Elders,* they then turn against tradition."

that sprung up so rankly under their culture. "When once they (the Arians) began to make new confessions of faith, belief became the creed of the times rather than of the gospels. Every year new creeds were made, and men did not keep to that simplicity of faith which they professed at their baptism. And then, what miseries ensued! for soon there were as many creeds as might please each party; and nothing else has been minded, since the council of Nice, but this creed-making.—New creeds have come forth every year, and every month: they have been changed, have been anathematized, and then re-established; *and thus, by too much inquiry into the faith, there is no faith left.* Recollect, too, that *there is not one of these heretics who does not impudently assert that all his blasphemies are derived from the Scriptures.*"—Ad Constant. lib. 2.

Having, from the earliest times of the Faith, such examples to warn them, and adhering firmly to the principle of *oneness* enjoined by Christ himself, the heads of the Church continued invariably to act upon the system of requiring all within the fold to follow the one Shepherd; and if any resisted or dissented, cast them forth from the flock. To this exclusion, no less awful a penalty was attached than the forfeiture of eternal salvation*; and, however stern and tremendous such a decree must appear, they who had been taught that there was but "one Lord, one faith, and one baptism," and who held, therefore, that he who was not in the ark must perish by the deluge, could not, with any sincerity, pronounce a more lenient sentence.

Under the shelter of such guards and sanctions, human as well as divine, has the Catholic Church been enabled to hold on her changeless course, and exhibit an example of permanence, indefectibility, and unity, to

---

* The Synodal epistle of the Council of Zerta, drawn up by St. Augustin, thus tells the Donatists:—" Whoever is separated from this Catholic Church, however innocently he may think he lives, for this crime alone, that he is separated from the Unity of Christ, will not have life, but the anger of God remains upon him."

which the whole history of human systems affords no parallel; sustaining herself, unblenched and unbroken—with the single exception of the partial schism of the Eastern Church—through a period commensurate with the existence of Christianity itself, and, amidst all the changes, eclipses, and wrecks of all other institutions, delivering down the same doctrines from father to son, through every age; while of all the leaders of sects opposed to her, from Simon Magus down to Luther, *not a single one has been able to frame a creed for his followers, the articles of which have remained unaltered beyond his own lifetime.*

CHAPTER XX.

A Dream.—Scene, a Catholic Church—time, the third century.—Angel of Hermas.—High Mass.—Scene shifts to Ballymudragget.—Rector's Sermon.—Amen Chorus.

This train of thought into which I had been led by the ceremonies of the morning, and which continued, more or less, to occupy me during the remainder of the day, was doubtless the cause of a strange dream by which I was visited that night, and which, for the benefit of all those who have any fancy for such " children of the idle brain," I shall here relate.

I found myself seated, as I thought, in the middle of a great church, in some foreign land, and, according to the impression I had on my mind, in the Third or Fourth Century. From the lights, the incense, and the sounds of psalmody that arose around, I could not doubt that I stood in some temple of Catholic worship, and, by a still greater miracle of fancy, was reconverted into a good, orthodox Catholic myself. On looking round, however, through the crowd of fellow-believers that encircled me, I was filled with astonishment at the varieties of hue and habit which they exhibited;—the Roman, the Carthaginian, the Gaul, the citizens of Athens and of Jerusalem, of Corinth and of Ephesus, the Alexandrian and the Spaniard, all seated round, arrayed in the different garbs of their respective countries, and waiting, in solemn silence, the opening of the Mass.

I now, for the first time, perceived, by my side, a youth of divine aspect, who regarded me with a smile of benevolence that came, like sunshine, into my heart. He was habited in the manner of a shepherd of the old pastoral times, and on considering his features more closely, I recognized in him the same friendly Angel who, in the garb of a Shepherd, had led Hermas through *his* series of Visions*. An exchange of salutations having

* See page 22 of this volume.

passed between us, I was about to inquire after his old pupil's celestial health, when he pressed his fore-finger on his lip, as a warning of silence, and, almost, at the same moment, the first words of the service broke on our ears. The venerable Priest who officiated seemed to my fancy a sort of compound being, made up from the descriptions I had read of some of the celebrated Fathers of the Church,—having the bald, Elisha-like head of St. Chrysostom, the upright eyebrows of St. Cyril, and "the beard prolix" (as Dr. Cave terms it) of the great St. Basil. Sometimes, too, as my dream shifted, like a morning mist, it appeared to me as if the holy personage ministering at the altar was no other than my good old confessor, Father O'H—— himself.

The public part of the mass being now ended, the moment had arrived when, by the solemn form of words, " Depart in peace," those who had not yet been initiated by baptism were warned to retire, and the Faithful left to perform the dread Sacrifice among themselves. But who shall worthily describe that rite which followed? Never shall I forget the effect, as it then presented itself to my fancy, of the still and unbreathing silence* of that vast multitude of Christians,—till, at the awful moment of communion, when, as the Priest, raising the sacred Host, pronounced it "the Body of Christ," the whole assembly fell prostrate, in adoration, before it, and the word " Amen†," as if with one voice and one soul, burst from all around. It was like a sweet and long-drawn peal of music, a concert of sounds, unbroken by a single breath of dissonance, from every quarter of this earth which the wind visits, —all blending in the belief of an incarnate

---

* When the Priest, says St. Chrysostom, stands before the Table, stretching out his hands to heaven, invocating the Holy Spirit, that he would come and give the contact, all is stillness and silence—πολλη ἡσυχια, πολλη σιγη.

† " In the very form of communion, the whole primitive Church made a solemn and public profession of the *truth* of the body of Christ in this Sacrament. The Priest, in giving it, spake these words, *Corpus Christi*, that is, *the body of Christ*, and the communicant answered *Amen*, that is, *it is true*."—Rutter on the Eucharist.

God, who by his flesh hath redeemed, and with his flesh still feeds, his creatures.

So overpowering was the effect of this sound upon me that I had nearly waked with emotion;—but the interruption was only momentary. Though the web of my dream had been broken, the thread was not altogether lost; and, after a short interval of entanglement, I found myself again in company with the Angel-Shepherd, in the very act of proposing to him, that, in return for his condescension in thus procuring me a peep into a church of the third century, he would allow me the honour of treating him to a similar glimpse into one of our new-fashioned churches, or conventicles, of the nineteenth.

Scarcely had the words passed my lips, when, by a sudden shift of scene, we were, at once, transported away to the Parish Church of Ballymudragget, and arrived just as the rich and roseate Rector of that place was ascending the pulpit, to read over to his half-a-sleep flock the last ready-made sermon he had purchased. The church appeared to me to have been, in some marvellous manner, enlarged for the occasion, and was now thronged with a dense multitude of persons whom, by that intuitive knowledge given only to dreamers, I knew to consist of all the various sects and denominations into which—with a vitality as infinitely divisible as that of the polypus itself—English Protestantism has been subdivided; and as, in the first stage of my dream, we had witnessed the spectacle of a variety of nations with one religion, so we now had before us the Reformed fashion of one nation with a variety of religions;—there being collected there (to mention but a few of the diversities of faith that presented themselves) Calvinists, Arminians, Antinomians, Independents, Baptists, Particular Baptists, Methodists, Kilhamites, Glassites, Haldanites, Bereans, Swedenborgians, Quakers, Shakers, Ranters, and Jumpers.

It was said of the great St. Ambrose that he had a peculiar talent for smelling out dead martyrs*; and no less quick a scent did my

---

* " Idem Præsul (says Daillé, gibingly, in speaking of the great Bishop of Milan's discovery of the two buried

friend, the Angel, appear to have for live heretics. For, perceiving instantly the difference between these moderns and the old, regular Christians he had been accustomed to, he begged, in a whisper, that I would explain briefly to him the particular form of heresy to which they belonged. The task was puzzling:—just as reasonably, indeed, might he have inquired of me the particular form and colour of the motes in a sunbeam. Not liking, however, to appear uncommunicative, I at once invented a generic name for the whole assembly, and told him the people he saw around us were Suists*,—so called, from following each his own way in religion, and only taking care in forming his peculiar creed, that it should as little as possible resemble the creed of his neighbour.

Saints, Gervasius and Protasius) quo nemo fuit in odorandis ac cernendis sub terrâ quantumvis altâ Reliquiis sagacior et acutior."

* " No common name being to be found, fit to comprehend our sectaries, but that of a Suist, one that follows his own dreams or fancy in choice of Scripture, and interpretation of it."—*Dr. Carier's Motives for Conversion to the Catholick Religion*, 1649.

Unluckily for this definition of mine, the discourse of the Reverend Rector happened to turn upon the one, only point on which his auditors were entirely unanimous,—namely, contempt and detestation for the ancient Catholic Church, its doctrines, observances, traditions, and teachers. To describe the astonishment of the Angel at the specimen of Ballymudragget Christianity now presented to him would be a task beyond my powers. When he heard the solemn words of our Lord in instituting the Eucharist, " Hoc est corpus," &c., profanely travestied into " *Hocus Pocus* * ;" when he was told gravely by the preacher that to maintain the corporal presence of Christ in the Sacrament is as absurd as to declare " an egg to be an elephant, or a musket-ball a pike †,"—I saw his celestial brow darken, at once, with sorrow and disdain, and he was only roused from

---

* It is no less a person than Tillotson who, in one of his writings, has descended to this ribaldry.

† " It might well seem strange if any man should write a book to prove that an egg is not an elephant and that a musket-ball is not a pike."—*Tillotson on Transubstantiation.*

the thoughtfulness into which such blasphemies plunged him on hearing the preacher mention Luther as the Apostle of this new Gospel he was expounding to them*. "Luther," muttered the Spirit to himself; and then, turning quick round to me, exclaimed, "Luther!— who is he?"

Somewhat startled to find the illustrious author of Protestantism so entirely unknown to my angelic friend, I proceeded to inform him of the few particulars I myself, at that time, knew of the great Reformer;— viz., that he was a monk of the order of St. Augustin who, about the year 1520, undertook to bring back the primitive purity of the Gospel;—that one of his first steps towards this object was to renounce his vows of chastity and marry a run-away nun whose views of reform, it appeared, coincided with his own;—that, still in furtherance of the

* The Reverend Preacher, however, had done injustice to Luther, who, as far as a belief in the Real Presence went (and without considering the *modus*), was perfectly orthodox.

same pious design, he struck up, as he himself informs us, an intimacy with the Devil; by whose friendly advice he pronounced the ancient Sacrifice of the Mass to be a nuisance, and abolished it accordingly*; that——I was thus, to the infinite wonder and horror of my companion, proceeding, when we both perceived that the portly Preacher had concluded his discourse; and all further communication between us was put an end to by the scene that followed.

Immediately on the conclusion of the Reverend gentleman's sermon, an Amen Chorus,—got up, it would appear, in direct opposition

---

* See Luther's own account of this famous conference, which he evidently believed himself to have held, with the Devil, on the subject of Private Masses, and the result of which was as above stated.—*De abrog. Miss. priv.* Had we not the recital of this strange illusion from the Reformer himself, who describes all particulars of the Devil's tone of voice, his off-hand manner of arguing, &c., such an instance of mental drivelling in so great a leader of human opinion would have been altogether inconceivable. He tells us, too, that his scenes of this kind, with the Devil, were frequent.—" Multas noctes mihi satis amarulentas et acerbas reddere ille novit."

to the symphonious strain we had heard some fifteen centuries before,—broke forth from the whole motley mass of Protestantism around us. Heavens, what a crash!—Not that celebrated pig-instrument, invented for the special amusement of Louis XV., could, with all its scale of grunts and squeaks multiplied a million-fold*, come, in the least degree, into comparison with the varieties of discord in which this general and prolonged Amen was uttered forth;—the deep, damnatory growl of the Calvinist, and the exclusive shriek of the Particular Baptist (shrill as the screaming of a sea-fowl in the storm) forming the treble

---

* A sort of instrument, played with keys like a harpsichord, or organ, invented, it is said, by some Abbé, for the amusement of Louis XV., in which pigs of different ages and tones, from the youngest to the oldest, were placed so as to form the treble and base of the scale. According as the performer played, a spike at the end of each key produced the tones desired, while a muzzle was so contrived as to act the part of damper, and stop the mouth of each pig as soon as his note was uttered. The whole was then covered in, so as to appear like an instrument, and the Abbé, it is stated, performed upon it, in the presence of the Court.

and base of this most discordant scale. Every moment, too, some new subdivision of dissonance was added to the original stock; till, at length, to so loud a pitch did the *charivari* swell, that no powers of sleeping, however dogged, could withstand it. In an instant, the whole visionary assemblage was put to flight; and, on awaking, I found myself lying, with one of the controversial volumes of the Rev. G. S. Faber, Rector of Long Newton, resting heavily on my chest. I had been employed in reading the volume when I dropped off to sleep, and its influence and superincumbence more than sufficiently accounted both for the long and deep slumber into which I was thrown, and the sort of Protestant nightmare under which I had awaked.

CHAPTER XXI.

Search after Protestantism suspended.—Despair of finding it among the Orthodox.—Resolve to try the Heretics.—Dead Sea of Learning.—Balance of Agreeableness between Fathers and Heretics.

I HAD, by this time, as my readers will easily believe, got not a little sick and weary of my search after Protestantism; a search hopeless, I found, as that of the Bramin, in the Eastern Tale, whose wife sent him all over the world, on a fool's errand, to look for the Fifth Volume of the Hindoo Scriptures*,—there never having been but *Four*. Tired of my learned studies and mortified to think how much time I had lost with them, I, for some weeks, gave up sullenly all thoughts of conversion, and was fast re-

* The *Tirrea Bede*, or Fifth Veda.—See, for this lively story, (a part of which closely resembles Chaucer's January and May) the collection called the *Bahardanush*.

lapsing into what the Abbé la Mennais calls *Indifferentism,* on the subject. It happened just then, however, that some circumstances connected intimately with that domestic secret to which I have so frequently alluded, but which must a little longer remain veiled in mystery, occurred to rouse me out of the listless apathy into which I had sunk, and make me feel that,—no matter what my scruples or convictions,—I must take to Protestantism, of *some* description or other, immediately.

The thought of finding, among the orthodox of the early Church, any creed but that of Popery was now, of course, out of the question. I had still, however, a fond hankering after those primitive ages, and knowing what power there is in antiquity to lend a grace to error, thought that if, even among the heretics of that venerable period, I could discover a little of the primæval Protestantism I had been looking for, it would be, at all events, no upstart heresy of a few centuries, but would, at least, have that degree of hoary heterodoxy about it which, if my conscience *must* give way, would throw dignity round its fall. Nor had I much fears of being disappointed in this object of my now crest-fallen ambition; for thus did I argue:—if the Catholic Church (as has been but too clearly demonstrated) held, in those early ages, the very same doctrines which she holds at present, those who, at that period, dissented from, or protested against, her doctrines must have been, in so far, Protestants; and though it does not always follow that two parties who differ with a third will agree with each other, yet was it natural to hope that among the grounds on which the Anti-Catholics of that time bottomed their heresies might be found some of those which have since furnished the basis of Protestantism. This glimpse of hope again awakened all my inquisitive energies; and, like a return of lost scent to the beagle, sent me once more, in full cry, after my game.

I have already remarked that the persevering Unity of Faith, which the Catholic Church has, through all ages, in pursuance of the Divine injunctions, maintained, could by no other device of human policy have been preserved than that which the See of Rome, as visible Head of the Christian world, has ever adopted,—namely, the repression of all private interpretation of Scripture, and the assertion to herself of the right of being at all times, and on all points of faith, the guide to truth, the expounder of Scripture, and the judge of controversy. "Truly," says Gregory of Nazianzum, in speaking of the mischiefs that arose from the exercise of private judgment,—"there should have been a law among us, whereby (as, among the Jews, young men were not allowed to read certain books of Scripture) not all men, and at all times, but certain persons only, and on certain occasions, should be permitted to discuss the points of Faith."—*Orat.* xxvi. St. Jerom, too, in a passage whose just sarcasm will be found to fit some of the Bible-expounders of the present day as closely as if they had been measured for it, thus speaks:—"In all menial arts there must be some one to show the way:—the art of understanding the Scriptures alone is open to every reader! Here, learned or unlearned, we can all interpret. The tattling old woman, the doting old man, the wordy sophist, all, all here presume; they tear texts asunder, and dare to become teachers before they have learned."—*Ep. L. T.* iv. *Pars.* 11.

To look for Protestantism—whose very corner-stone is the right of private judgment,—in a Church whose system it has been, from the first, to acknowledge no such right, was, I now perceived, a gross mistake,—a mistake into which nothing but my entire ignorance of the Rule of Faith prescribed to the Primitive Christians could have led me. For, after all, in this point,—in the latitude given to private interpretation,—lies the broad and essential distinction between the Catholic Church and her opponents, under whatever forms or at whatever periods such opponents may have appeared. The test, indeed, is as true and as applicable to the respective parties in the first century as in the nineteenth; and in whatever age, however early, we find professed Christians, questioning or rejecting the authority of the Church, and grounding their opposition to her rites or doctrines upon the Scriptures, as interpreted by themselves, we may be assured that *there* is already at work the spirit of Protestantism.

Having come to this conclusion, I now, once more, betook myself to my folios,—once more plunged into that Dead Sea of Learning which is so little suited to a diver of light bulk, like myself*, and over which never hath the wing of Fancy been known to fly without drooping. It is true, my present course of study lay through a far more varied line of road than that by which I had before travelled. In my researches hitherto, I had kept chiefly to what the Fathers call "the Royal Road of Orthodoxy;"—whereas I was

---

* In explanation of these metaphors of my young friend, I may as well state, that the difficulty of diving in the Dead Sea was noticed as far back as Strabo's time; and that the effect of its exhalations on birds that fly over it is a common but, I believe, unfounded notion.

now about to track Heresy through her by-lanes and cross-ways; to beat up, as it were, the haunts of Heterodoxy, and ascertain to what extent Protestantism had burrowed among her coverts. As far as amusement goes, my readers will be, I should hope, gainers by this change of route. Good company, says a French *roué*, is a good thing, but bad is better; and just so did I find the balance of agreeableness between my Fathers and my Heretics,—the respectability being all, of course, on the former side, while the amusement is on the latter; there being, in fact, no conceivable freak or vagary of opinion into which, at the early periods of the Church I am about to speak of, that will-o'-th'-wisp, Private Judgment, did not lure his weak followers.

CHAPTER XXII.

The Capharnaites the first Protestants.—Discourse of our Saviour at Capernaum—its true import.—Confirmatory of the Catholic doctrine of the Eucharist.

It is melancholy to think how soon Heresy intruded itself into the Christian fold; and how, in the same manner as the blessed abode of our first Parents was scarce called into existence before the Spirit of Evil contrived to enter and darken it with his doubts, so Christianity had hardly opened her second Eden to mankind, before the same Evil intruder, with the same tongue of reasoning and heart of guile, came to question her mysteries and throw a blight over her blessings.

One of the first instances, and by far the most signal, that occur in the History of Christianity, of this sort of questioning spirit, this rising up of the judgment against Faith, to which all the Heresies and Schisms that have occurred since owe their rise, is to be found in the memorable speech of the Jews of Capernaum, when our Saviour first announced the great mystery of the Eucharist:—" How can this man give us his flesh to eat?"

We have here, I repeat, one of the first recorded protests of Private Judgment against the mysteries of the Church of Christ. It is, therefore, of importance to examine a little into the details of the great transaction it refers to; and we shall find, I think, that could the various texts of Scripture levelled against " the wisdom of this world" have left us any room to doubt of the infinitely low estimate at which human reason and its conclusions are rated in the eyes of heaven, the little deference paid by Christ, on this occasion, to the reasoning powers of his auditors would be, in itself, a sufficient evidence of the humbling truth; would, of itself, sufficiently teach the presumptuous Spirit of Private Judgment how sacredly the precincts of Faith are meant to be guarded from its intrusions.

Our Saviour had told them, " the bread which I will give you is my flesh, which I will give for the life of the world." Had the hearers of these words understood them to have been used metaphorically by the speaker, neither wonder nor scandal could possibly have resulted from them. But it is evident the whole assembly understood his language literally, and while the Apostles were silent and, with implicit faith, " believed on him that God had sent," the Jews and many even of his own disciples murmured at such hard doctrine. We can even imagine, at that juncture, some Capharnaite divine, some Tillotson of the Synagogue, thus addressing his flock:— " Surely, my beloved brethren, it can never enter into any of our minds that this man will literally hold himself in his hand, an give away himself, from himself, with his own hands*." With far more grounds and

---

* See Tillotson, on Transubstantiation, whose words are here repeated verbatim. It is not a little curious that the representation which Tillotson gives of this miracle, for the purpose of throwing ridicule on it, is the same that the

decency, indeed, might the Capharnaites have urged such an objection, seeing that they interpreted the promised eating of the Lord's body in a carnal sense; even so much so (says St. Augustin) as to suppose that he meant to cut up his own flesh in bits and distribute it among believers*.

The Redeemer saw what was passing in

Fathers did not hesitate to put forward as an enhancement and proof of its stupendous nature. Thus St. Augustin, in a passage already cited,—" When, committing to us his body, he said, This is my body, *Christ was held in his own hands.*" " Our Lord gave his body (says St. James of Nisibis), *with his own hands,* for food."

* " Many who were present, not understanding this, were scandalized; for, hearing him, they thought of nothing but their own flesh. He therefore said, 'the flesh profiteth nothing;' that is, it profiteth nothing, as they understood it; for they understood it to mean flesh, as it is in a dead body, or as it is sold in the market, not as animated by life."—*August. Tract.* 27.

It is supposed by other divines that these words, " the flesh profiteth nothing, it is the spirit that quickeneth," had reference rather to the agency of the Holy Spirit, by whose descent upon the elements, according to the belief of the early Church, their transformation into the body of Christ was effected, and the vivifying virtue communicated to them.

their minds, as well as in those of his disciples*,—who, however less gross and carnal

* In remarking upon the exclamation of the Jews—" How can this man give us his flesh to eat?" Cyril of Alexandria says, " They reflected not that *nothing is impossible with God*. But if thou, O Jew, continuest yet to urge this *How*, I will ask *thee how* the rod of Moses was changed into a serpent? *how* the waters were changed into the nature of blood? . . . . For our parts, let us derive great instruction from the iniquity of others; and cherishing a firm faith on these mysteries, let us never, on so sublime a point, either in words express, or in thoughts entertain, this *How*."—Com. in Joan.

The following declaration, drawn up by St. Cyril and approved by the Third General Council, may be considered as conveying the belief of the Catholic Church on this subject:—" We receive it (the Eucharist) not as common flesh: far be this thought from us; nor as the flesh of a sanctified man, and united to the Word by an equality of honour, or as having obtained a divine inhabitation; *but we receive it as the truly vivifying and own flesh of the Word made man*. For as the Word, as God, is essentially life, the moment it became one with its flesh, it imparted to this flesh a vivifying virtue. Wherefore, although Christ said—' Unless you eat the flesh of the Son of Man and drink his blood, you shall not have life in you' (John, vi. 54), we are not to imagine that it is the flesh of a man like to ourselves, but *truly the flesh of him* (ιδιαν αληθως γενομενην) who for us was made and was called the Son of Man."

might have been their notion of the mystery, not the less murmured at its incomprehensibility, and, in consequence, meditated that secession from their Master, of which they were afterwards guilty*. Here then was the important moment—important to all eternity, —when, the divine teacher and his disciples being confronted with each other, the question between Reason and Faith, between Private Judgment and Authority, was, for the guidance of future ages, to be brought solemnly to a decision. Here assuredly was the moment when, if Christ had not truly and really meant what he had spoken,—when, if there had been any figure of speech or allegory in his words, on whose correct interpretation no less a stake than the eternal life of mankind depended, he had not only an opportunity but, if I may venture so to say, was bound by the conditions of his high mission, to explain away any such perilous ambiguity; nor, mysterious as was the nature of the sacrament itself, to leave also the need-

---

* "From that time many of his disciples went back and walked no more with him."—John, vi. 66.

less mist of metaphor hanging over it. If, in short, to conciliate human reason, by smoothing away difficulties which must, to the end of time, he knew, startle and alienate the " weak in faith,"—if any such deference to human doubts and judgments ever entered, but in the remotest degree, into his purposes, then, I repeat, would have been the moment for him to evince such deference, and by so doing authorize the jurisdiction of Reason over Faith for ever after.

But *did* our Lord thus act? *did* he, indeed, show any such consideration for the judgment of his hearers, or attempt, in the slightest degree, to explain or soften down his own startling announcement? Did he (as has been done *for* him, in modern times,) confess that, on so solemn an occasion, he had made use of a most forced and unnatural metaphor, and that, by eating his flesh and drinking his blood, he meant nothing more than believing his doctrine? *Did* " the great Proclaimer" of this miracle endeavour to fritter away its wonders, and bring them down to the low level of the faith of his hearers, by averring, in the language of the Sacramentarians, that the bread and wine were but the signs or symbols of his body, or by assuring them, with the Calvinists, that it was by a mere act of faith they were to partake of his flesh, while the body itself would be, at the time, as remote from them as heaven was from the altar? *Did* our Saviour, I ask, do thus? Let the sacred text answer the question. So far from offering such explanations,—any one of which would have sufficiently diluted away the difficulties of the doctrine to render it easy and palatable to the stubborn judgment of his auditors,—the Divine Master, as if to show how easily he could " bring to nothing the understandings of the prudent," deigned no otherwise to answer their objections or their murmurs than by repeating, in still more emphatic language, the declaration that had so astounded them:—" Verily, verily*, I say

---

* It is supposed by some that the word Amen, as repeated here, is a positive oath; and Basnage is, if I recollect right, one of the authorities for its having been

unto you, except ye eat of the flesh of the Son of Man, and drink his blood, ye have no life in you."

The whole conduct, indeed, and language of our Saviour, throughout this most memorable scene, stands as an eternal rebuke to the presumption of human Reason, in its vain attempt to fathom such " heavenly things;" while the awful announcement then made of the miraculous Feast about to be instituted*,

employed in that sense by the Jews. However this may be, the word, doubtless, imports a very high degree of asseveration; and " to suppose (as Johnson remarks) that our Saviour used it only to justify a very catechrestical expression is to suppose that a wise and humble teacher was so fond of a figure as, for the sake of it, to give occasion to his hearers to desert him."

In the curious Conference represented to have passed between Charles I. and the Marquis of Worcester at Ragland, the latter, in remarking on the opinion of those who suppose Christ to have spoken figuratively on this occasion, says justly, " There would not have been so much difficulty in the *belief* if there had not been more in the *mystery;* there would not have been so much offence taken at a *memorandum,* nor so much stumbling at a *figure.*"

* So far were the ancient Christians from supposing

followed up, as it was, on the solemn night of Institution, by those simple and irrefragable words, " This is my Body*," form the grounds of that implicit Catholic belief, which the Church of Christ has, at all times, maintained, and which, however Capharnaites may still scoff, and loose disciples still murmur, will never, as long as the one Catholic Church endures, pass away.

that our Saviour instituted so momentous and wonderful a rite without any announcement, any preparation of the minds of his followers for such an event, that they accounted naturally for the calmness with which the Apostles heard the awful words of institution by the previous knowledge of the nature of the Sacrament which Christ had, in his discourse (John vi.), communicated to them. Thus St. Chrysostom:—" He transferred them to another banquet; a banquet most tremendous, saying, 'Take, eat, this is my body.' How was it that they were not seized with terror, when they heard this? Because he had previously discoursed with them at large upon the subject."—*Homil.* lxxxii. *in Matt.*

* " Let us not break (said Gaudentius) that *most solid bone,* ' This is my body—this is my blood;' but if any thing remain in it which individuals do not understand, let it be burnt away by the ardent fire of Faith."—*Tractat.* ii. *de Pasch.*

CHAPTER XXIII.

The Docetæ, the earliest heretics.—Denial of the Real Presence.—Simon Magus and his Mistress.—Simon a Protestant.—Delight at the discovery.—The Ebionites.—The Elcesaites.

Thus far I had been as fully successful in my new line of search as I could desire,—having found that great and leading principle of Protestantism, the right of private judgment, starting, as it were, into existence almost coevally with the birth-hour of our faith, and making the first trial of its strength against the living words of our Saviour himself. We have next to consider the workings of the same headstrong principle, as manifested in the various heresies that rose against his Church; and it is not a little remarkable that the very first sect of heretics we meet with, the first instance of dissent from Catholicity on record, should turn on the same trying point that had already called forth the "*How*" of the Capharnaites,—that point which, as from the first it has been a stone of stumbling to the weak in faith, so will it continue, I have no doubt, to be a test of the true believer in Christ's words to the last. The sect with whom this *Mother* Heresy originated, was that of the Docetæ, already mentioned,—a branch of the Gnostic Christians, nearly as old as Christianity itself, who gave as their reason for refusing to join in worship with the orthodox, that they *could not acknowledge the bodily presence of Christ in the Eucharist**.

* It was but by some branches of the Docetæ that the Eucharist was rejected; the greater number of them appear to have celebrated it, but only in the Protestant sense, as a mere type or emblem :—" Professant tous le Doketisme, les Gnostiques qui conservoient la Cêne n'enseignerent jamais l'union réelle de l'homme avec la chair ou le sang du Sauveur; cet acte qu'ils célébraient en présence de leurs catéchumènes et qu'ils rangaient dans la catégorie des choses exotériques, *n'étoit pour eux que l'emblême de leur union mystique avec un être appartenant au Plérome.*"—*Hist. du Gnosticisme.*

To the Marcionites of the next age, who had also their Eucharist,—though believing, with the Docetæ, that Christ's body was but apparent,—it was urged as an argument, both

Thus do errors, like comets, come and go, while Truth, like the sun, remains always stationary. Though the grounds on which these heretics denied the Real Presence were different, of course, from those on which it was rejected by Protestants fifteen hundred years after, yet was the result they arrived at precisely the same;—insomuch, that could one of those Gnostic Christians now reappear upon earth, he would find nothing in the unreal and figurative Presence, maintained by Church of England divines, that could, in the slightest degree, offend his most anti-corporeal notions, or prevent him from being conscientiously a partaker of their Sacrament.

At last, therefore, I had the pleasure of finding myself in something like good Protestant company; and, knowing that to the heretic, Simon Magus, is attributed the high honour of being the head of the whole family

by Irenæus and Tertullian, that in owning the Sacrament of the body and blood, they confuted their own opinion. Will it *still*, after all this, be contended that the ancient Christians did not believe in the *Reality* of the Presence?

of Gnostic Christians, I proceeded forthwith to inform myself of all such particulars as are known concerning the parent of so worthy a progeny. Undoubtedly, wherever the presumption of human judgment is the theme, this Arch-Heretic has a paramount claim to be remembered,—seeing that he pretended to understand Christianity better than Christ himself. There are, indeed, some curious coincidences between his career and that of the Arch-parent of the Protestant Reformation, to which, though at the risk of appearing illiberal, I cannot help adverting. One of his first steps, for instance, in setting himself up against Christ, was to take a young female companion to be the enlivener of his ministry, —declaring (with a flight beyond Luther) that he himself was the incarnate Power, and his mistress the incarnate Wisdom, of God*.

* This lady's name was Helena; and, among the various steps of that descending scale of transmigration through which she was represented to have passed, before she sank into the capacity of Simon's concubine, she had had the honour, it was said, of being, in her time, no less a personage than that celebrated Helen whose beauty provoked the War of Troy.

Another point in which it may be said that the two Reformers resembled each other lay in the alliance formed by both with " the *nether* empire;" Simon Magus being well known to have had demons for his familiars*, and the famous conference between Luther and *his* Devil, on the subject of the Mass, being, as is well known, one of the most memorable events of that great Reformer's life †.

Having satisfied myself thus far, as to the *practice* of Simon, I lost no time in inquiring

---

* Hence the Magia Demoniaca, or Black Art, is traced to Simon as its inventor. It is but fair, however, to say that some learned persons have doubted whether the Simon mentioned in the Acts of the Apostles was the same with the Heresiarch of the Gnostic Sects. Among others, the learned Frieslander, Vitringa, is of opinion that they were two different persons.

† It is amusing to observe the irritation which any allusion to this famous colloquy is sure to produce in the temper of most Protestant controvertists. Unable to get rid of Luther's own statement of the matter, all that they have for it is to deny stoutly that this conference had any influence on his opinions concerning the Mass. We are, indeed, assured gravely by Claude and others, that Luther had both written and spoken publicly against the sacrifice of the Mass two years before any of these suggestions of the Devil were made to him.

into the nature of his *doctrine;* and it may be imagined with what pleasure, on opening the pages of the historian, Theodoret, I discovered the following passage :—" He (Simon Magus) ordered those who believed in him not to attend to the Prophets, nor to fear the threats of the Law, but to do, as free persons, whatever they wished; *for that they would obtain salvation, not by Good Works, but by Grace*.*" Here was, at last, Protestantism, in its fullest perfection,—the very principle, in fact, on which the authors of the Reformation first started, however their followers, and even some of themselves, saw reason to shrink from its consequences afterwards;—here was the same Antinomian spirit which dictated the declaration of the Lutherans in 1557, that good works are *not* necessary to salvation†; —and here was the basis also of Calvin's *in-*

---

* Ου δια πραξεων αγαθων αλλα δια χαριτος τευξισθαι της σωτηριας.—Hær. Fab.

† At the conference held, by order of Charles V., at Worms. We know that Amsdorf, a warm disciple of Luther, even went so far as to maintain that *Good Works were an obstacle to salvation.*

amissible grace, which renders even the worst works no obstacle to the eternal blessedness of the Elect. So rejoiced was I to light, at last, on a sample of genuine Protestantism,—from the same source, too, where the denial of Christ's bodily Presence originated *—that I could not help breaking out in the language of Ulysses, when he, at length, found himself in sight of Ithaca, after all his wanderings,—

Χαιρ' Ιθακη, μετ' αιθλα, μετ' αλγεα πικρα
Ασπασιως τεον ουδας ικανομαι.

or, as I translated it, at the moment, in my rapture,—

Hail, Faith of Protestants!—thou home
To which so long I've sigh'd to come.
To seek thee need no longer plague us,
Thou'rt found, at last, in——Simon Magus.

---

* From Simon the doctrine of the Docetæ, or Phantastics, took its origin:—" Quoniam Christum Dominum (says Le Grand, under the head of Simon) non veram carnem assumpsisse, nec ejusdem cum nostra naturæ esse profitebatur, ejusdem in Eucharistia præsentiam confiteri nolebat.—*Ignatius ap. Theodoret. Dial.* 3."

It may be suspected, perhaps, that one of the chief ingredients of my satisfaction at this discovery was the malicious pleasure it gave to certain Popish feelings, still stirring within me, at being thus able to trace two of the most elemental and vital doctrines of Protestantism to such a source as Simon Magus; and I had, myself, I confess, certain misgivings as to the mixture of some such leaven with my joy. Resolving, therefore, to be generous, I repressed at once all unworthy triumph, and thinking it better even to go without Protestantism altogether than to come by it in this suspicious and disreputable manner, I dismissed Simon Magus entirely from my mind, and hastened on in quest of some more respectable creed-master.

Never yet has there been an extreme opinion started in this world, that there was not an opposite extreme ready to start at the same time. Thus, to the Docetæ, who held that Christ was entirely divine, there was opposed a counter-heresy, that of the Ebionites, who held, with the Protestant Unitarians, that he was merely human. It was, indeed, by dividing the double nature of our Saviour between them that these two sects contrived to make out their two heresies,—the Docetæ allowing that he was God, but not man*, and the Ebionites contending that he was Man, not God.

Akin to the Ebionites†, in maintaining the simple humanity of the Saviour, were the Elcesaites, a sect of heretics, half Jews, half Christians, and (if not very much misrepresented) entire maniacs. As if to make up to Christ for depriving him of his divinity, they attributed to him a human form ninety-six miles long, and twenty-four broad ; and this measurement they considered themselves authorized to make

---

* Some of those Gnostics who held that Christ wore only the appearance of man got over the difficulties of the crucifixion, as they thought, by saying that, on the way to Mount Calvary, he changed shapes with Simon of Cyrene, who carried the cross, and that Simon was the person really crucified by the Jews, while Christ stood by, invisibly, laughing at their mistake.

† It was the opinion of the Ebionites that God had given the empire of all things to two persons, Christ and the Devil; that the Devil had full power over the present world, and Christ over the world to come.—*Fleury, Hist. Ecclesiast.*

by the words of St. Paul (Ephes. iii. 18), where he exhorts Christians to be " able to comprehend, with all Saints, what is the breadth, and length, and depth, and height," of Christ. The Holy Ghost they supposed to be a female, and of much the same dimensions as Christ; and the learned reason they gave for this peculiar notion of the Spirit's sex was that *Raouah*, the term in Hebrew for the Holy Ghost, is of the feminine gender; besides (added these *reasoning* Christians), the inconvenience of having two Fathers for Christ is, by this interpretation, avoided.

Notwithstanding these blasphemous absurdities, the descendants of the man, from whom the sect was named, continued through a long course of time to be honoured as " the Blessed Race," and, so late as the reign of Valens, we hear of two sisters of this hallowed breed being held in such extravagant veneration by the people, that not only the dust from their feet but even the spittle from their mouths were caught up with enthusiasm by the crowd and preserved in boxes as a charm against all ills.

CHAPTER XXIV.

Scriptural learning of the Gnostics—their theories.—Account of the system of the Valentinians.—Celestial Family.—Sophia—her daughter.—Birth of the Demiurge.—Bardesanes.

To those who have observed how invariably, throughout the history of Christianity, the multiplication of heresies, schisms, and innovations in faith has been, at all times, in direct proportion to the diffusion of the Scriptures among the people, it will afford no surprise to learn that the Gnostic heretics, by whom such a flood of fantastic errors was let loose in the first ages, were of all the Christians of that period the most versed in Scripture, and the most laborious in quest of texts to suit their mischievous purposes*. So industrious, indeed, are they known to have

---

* " Il n'est guère d'opinion dans leurs riches théories qu'ils n'aient taché d'appuyer de quelques passages des Ecritures."—*Histoire du Gnosticisme.*

been in this line of research, that, notwithstanding the blasphemies and extravagances with which their writings abounded, Erasmus mourns, as a biblical scholar, over the loss of the works, on account of the wonderful stores of scriptural knowledge which they contained.

To such as hold, in direct opposition to the Catholics, that the Sacred Volume cannot be too widely thrown open,—who call out for the Bible, the whole Bible, and nothing but the Bible for all classes of readers, it may not be uninstructive to produce some examples of the use heretofore made of this privilege, and more particularly to show what were the recondite truths and mysteries which those learned searchers of the Sacred Volume, the Gnostics, professed to find in its pages.

To enter into any detailed exposition of the various systems which these heretics put forth, —each new system but presenting a different modification of the same Magian theory of the Two antagonist Principles*,—would be a

---

* These principles they called the Two Roots: δυο ριζας οιδα, πονηραν και αγαθην.—*Dial. de recta fide.*

task far beyond my present purpose. The solution of the great problem of the Origin of Evil was the object at which all these elaborate and, in some few instances, poetical inventions aimed; and, in most of them, the theory of a Good and an Evil Principle is combined with the notion, also Eastern, of certain spiritual existences or Æons, supposed to have proceeded by emanation from the one Supreme Fountain of Being*. In the system of Valentinus, however, of which I am about to give some account, this process of Emanation was, under the sanction of the doctrine of Christ's Sonship, exchanged for that of Generation; and how prodigal was the use made by the heresiarch of this orthodox precedent the following sketch of his system, collected from Irenæus and other writers on ancient heresies, will show.

He supposed the unknown and inaccessible Father to have dwelt, from all eternity, in

* This perfect Æon, existing before all things, they described as dwelling on some "invisible and unnameable heights:" εν αορατοις και ακατονομαστοις υψωμασι.—Irenæus.

silence and repose, accompanied only by a certain Power, or Intelligence, that served him as consort, and by which, or whom, in the fulness of time, he produced a son and daughter, bearing the names of Nous and Aletheia. This pair, in their turn, gave being to another couple called Logos and Zoe, and these again to a fourth pair, Anthropos and Ecclesia. All these eight Æons he pretended to find expressly named in the opening verses of the Gospel of St. John.

This process of spiritual procreation having been thus carried on, couple after couple, through fifteen generations, the number of Thirty spiritual beings, or Æons, came at last to be collected, forming altogether that Pleroma, or Plenitude, of spiritual existence, to which St. Paul, said these heretics, clearly alludes in the Epistle to the Colossians, i. 19. —" For it pleased the Father that in him all Fulness should dwell." The exact number, too, of Thirty Æons is, said they, manifestly figured by the thirty years of his life during which Christ remained concealed from the world.

Of the last born of the fifteen couples that composed this celestial family, the female, whose name was Sophia, or Wisdom, happened, by some accident or other, to slip out of the Pleroma into infinite space; and there, alone and bewildered, would infallibly, it is supposed, have been lost, had not Horus, who seems to have acted as a sort of watchman of the Pleroma, gone in quest of the stray Spirit and brought her safe back again. She had, however, during her short absence from home, given birth to a daughter, who, though spiritual like her mother, was, from the peculiar circumstances under which she was born, and her exclusion from the bright region of the Pleroma, unformed and degenerate. The fall of this twelfth Æon (Sophia) is, they allege, marked out in the fall of Judas, the twelfth apostle, as well as by the disease of the woman, in Matthew ix. 20, which had lasted twelve years, and which the power of Christ, like that of Horus, stopped and healed.

In the mean time, Nous,—by the especial foresight of the Father, who wished to guard against any diminution of the Æon family by the occurrence of such another accident as had happened to the Sophia,—added a new couple of Beings, male and female, to their community, namely, Christ and the Holy Ghost, by whom the security of the Pleroma and the union of its heavenly occupants was ratified. From Christ they all learned to know the Father, or, rather, were taught to content themselves with knowing that he is incomprehensible; while by the Holy Spirit they were instructed how to laud this great Being and to dwell together in perfect unity and repose. In testimony of their gratitude for this state of blessedness, the Æons agreed, with the full consent of the Father, to produce, among themselves, by joint contribution, Jesus, or the Saviour,—each furnishing towards the production of this new Being whatever was most exquisite in their own natures, so as to render him the flower of the whole Pleroma,—and hence is it (said the Valentinians) that St. Paul declares of Jesus, the Saviour, that " in him dwelleth all the Fulness of the Godhead."

While within the Pleroma all this joy prevailed, in the dismal region without, the poor offspring of Sophia (herself distinguished by the name of Sophia-Achamoth) was left, a formless abortion, to wander through the void. Once, pitying her distress, Christ stretched forth his cross to aid her; but though his touch gave form and life, it imparted not science, and, accordingly, still was the lone outcast abandoned to her fate, experiencing all the misery of desire without knowledge, and left a prey to the various passions of sadness, fear, and anguish, which have since become the lot of the humanity that sprung from her.

In this state of suffering she, at last, turned to him who gave her life, and that one movement of conversion changed her whole fate. Sent graciously down by Christ to her aid, the Saviour came attended by his angels, and releasing her from the yoke of the passions, without altogether extinguishing them, bestowed upon her at last the long-desired gift of knowledge. Her look of joy, we are told, at this deliverance was felt through all Chaos, and from that first smile of Sophia Achamoth the origin of light is to be dated. From this moment, too, began that series of creative and pro-creative operations by which this world and all that it contains was produced. The various offsprings, spiritual, psychic, and material, to which Sophia and her new friends, the angels, gave birth between them, it is not easy to describe and still less so to understand. Suffice it to say, that out of this commerce sprung that inferior God, or Demiurge, by whom, according to all the Gnostic sects, this visible world was created.

Such was the fanciful account given by Valentinus of the events that happened, as he supposed, in the world of the Unknown Father, before the creation of this;—such the wild tissue of fiction which its inventor boasted to have derived from the secret communications of Christ himself to his apostles, and which was, strange to say, adopted by a large portion of the Christian world, extending even into Gaul and Spain, during the second and third centuries*.

Had we only the vague and forced applications of Scripture by which the Valentinians supported this fantastic theology to assist us in judging of the Gnostics†, as interpreters of Holy Writ, our opinion of their ingenuity in this line must have fallen far short of their reputation. Of the speculations, however, of some of their other sects enough has been preserved,—more particularly of the Marcionites, on the subject of the Old Testament,—to show that, in applying their wild theories to Scripture, they were at least suffi-

---

* It was not till towards the beginning of the fifth century that the Valentinians may be said to have dwindled away. Gregory of Nazianzum, who died towards the close of the fourth, represents them as then among the almost extinguished sects.

† " Ces allegories et ces personifications se comprenaient encore parfaitement au second siècle de notre ère ; cependant, dès que les docteurs orthodoxes se furent séparés distinctement des partisans de la Gnose, ils leur en firent des objets de reproche ; et S. Ephrem ne rapporte qu'en tremblant le blasphême de Bardesanes, qui osoit donner deux filles au Saint Esprit."—*Histoire du Gnosticisme.*

ciently acute to be mischievous; and, above all, to show at what an early period an opening was made for infidelity by the adoption of that proud, Protestant principle, the right of Private Judgment, and the desertion, in consequence, of those only true and safe guides, the Apostolical Traditions and the Authority of the Church.

Through all the other Gnostic sects the same system of Æonogony prevailed, the points of difference between their theories lying more in the details than in the principle. Thus Bardesanes, though adopting the same notion as to the succession of the Æons by syzygies or couples, yet so far changed the order of their genealogy as to make Christ the immediate son of the Father, by that companion whom he had, in the silence of his solitude, created unto himself. Next after Christ, too, in the order of being, came the sister and spouse of Christ, the Holy Ghost; and a union having taken place between these spiritual personages, two daughters, we are told, named Maio and Sabscho, were their offspring.

CHAPTER XXV.

The Gnostics, believers in Two Gods.—The Creator and the Unknown Father.—Their charges against the Jehovah of the Jews.—Marcion—his Antitheses.—Apelles.—Belief in Two Saviours.—Hatred of the Jewish Code.—Ophites.—Marriage of Jesus with Sophia Achamoth.

However differing from each other in the superstructures of their respective theories, there was one fundamental principle upon which Valentinians, Marcionites, Basilidians, &c., all built, namely, that the God of the Old Testament, whom they held to be the Creator of this world, is a wholly different being from the God of the New;—the latter being, according to them, the Unknown and unapproachable Father, of whom Christ was the son, and by whom, in his mercy and goodness, Christ was sent down to earth, to repair the evils which the Demiurge, or Creator, had caused. In support of this bold theory they refer to the contrast, both in spirit and precept, which is so strikingly, they allege, exhibited between the Law and the Gospel, and maintain it to be impossible to believe that both could come from the same hand. While the Being revealed by the Saviour, said they, is a God of Mercy and Love, the Jehovah, or Demiurge, was a God ignorant, unjust, vindictive, and inconsistent.

Of the ignorance of the Jehovah, one of the instances they give is his not knowing where Adam was, when he sought him in the garden, nor whether he had yet eaten of the forbidden tree. " And the Lord God called unto Adam, and said unto him, Where art thou? . . . . . hast thou eaten of the tree?' But, though most of their articles of impeachment against the Creator are either thus frivolous, or fanciful, there are some that have appeared sufficiently acute and searching to be thought worthy of revival by modern infidels. For instance, his incapacity, they say, as a Creator, was manifestly proved by his having so ill-performed his task in creating Man, as to be forced to repent him of his work, and even to resolve on destroying all living things (Genesis, vi. 6, 7). The advice given by him to his chosen people, on their departure from Egypt, to despoil the Egyptians of their valuables, under the pretence of borrowing them, was the ground of another of those daring charges against the God of the Jews, in which these heretics but anticipated the profane scoffs of Voltaire and his followers. In ridiculous consistency, too, with the name Καθαροι, or *Puritans*, which, like some modern Protestants, a few of these sects assumed, one of the minor faults they objected to the Jehovah was, his habit of *swearing*, and—what appears to have been, in their eyes, an aggravation of the offence—swearing by *himself*. The only merit, indeed, they seemed inclined to allow to this Being was that of candour as to his own evil-doings,—he himself having, as they said, acknowledged, through his organ, Isaiah (xlv. 7), that darkness and evil were the work of his hands.

It was in support of this peculiar view of the two dispensations that the Gnostic chief,

Marcion, exerted particularly, as I have already said, his acumen and zeal. To show how opposite were the characters of the Jewish and the Christian God, and how much at variance with each other, in spirit, are the Law and the Gospel, this heretic drew up what he called " Antitheses*," in which the precepts of the two codes are brought in contrast with each other. Observe, said he, the difference;—by the Creator the principle of fierce retaliation is inculcated, " eye for eye and tooth for tooth" (Exod. xxi. 24), while by the Saviour we are forbidden to return even an insult (Luke, vi. 29). Jesus cured the blind (John, ix.);—David, on the contrary, hated and ill-treated them (2 Samuel, v. 8). The Messenger of the Supreme God suffered little children to come unto him, and blessed

* It would appear that this sort of antithetical comparison was a favourite weapon with the heretics even in St. Paul's time, who warns Timothy to avoid the ἀντιθέσεις τῆς ψευδωνόμου γνώσεως—" the antitheses of the falsely-named Gnosis, or Gnosticism;" for such, it appears to me, ought to be the translation of the words, and not, as now, " oppositions of science falsely so called."

them (Mark, x. 14, 16);—the messenger of the Creator cursed them, and gave them to be devoured by bears (2 Kings, ii. 24).

With some ingenuity, too, he cited, as confirmatory of his doctrine, the following verse from St. Paul's Second Epistle to the Corinthians:—" In whom *the God of this world* hath blinded the minds of them which believe not, lest the light of the glorious Gospel of Christ, who is the image of God, should shine unto them." By " the God of this world" is to be understood, said Marcion, the Demiurge, or Creator, in contradistinction to the good God, or Father of Jesus Christ, who is the God of the Christians. So dangerously strong in his favour was this passage considered, that, in order to evade its force, Tertullian and Irenæus were for putting a comma after " God," so as to separate it from the words, " of this world," and thus strain the structure of the sentence to the following meaning:—" In whom God hath blinded the minds of the unbelievers of this world."

That Christ himself meant to establish an

opposition between the old and new order of things appears clearly, this heretic said, from his discourses against the Law and the Prophets, and such allusions to the incompatibility of the two dispensations as are conveyed in those sayings, " no man putteth wine in old bottles," and " no man can serve two masters." A similar allusion to the Law and the Gospel he professed to find in the words of the Apostle, " the letter killeth, but the spirit giveth life," which mean clearly, he maintained, that the code of Moses left man in death, ignorance, and vice, while the sublime revelation of the Christos imparts the Pneuma, or breath, of Divine life.

He found also, as he thought, a precedent for his antithetical theory in the language held by St. Paul to the Judaizing Christians, and in the contrast drawn by that Apostle between the Jewish and Christian Dispensations, as being, the former but a type, the latter the substance;—the one transitory and peculiar, the other universal and permanent.

When once, in religion, a departure from

the right line commences, each succeeding step but increases the deviation;—and this was remarkably exemplified in the course of all the successors of these ancient heresiarchs. Apelles, one of the disciples of Marcion, improved upon the daring criticism of his master, and in a work similar to the Antitheses, to which he gave the name of Syllogisms, not only brought forth again all the alleged contradictions between the Old and New Testaments, but laboured to point out such inconsistencies and contrarieties between different parts of the Hebrew Scriptures themselves as, if proved, must have considerably weakened, if not entirely overturned their authority *.

One of the most instructive lessons we learn, perhaps, from history is to know that

* The very same system has been pursued by Voltaire, in his attacks on the Old Testament (See *Diction. Philosoph.* &c.):—" En effet (says the author of the *Histoire du Gnosticisme*) Marcion articula contre les codes et les institutions Judaiques plus d'accusations ou, si l'on veut, plus de blasphêmes qu'il n'en est sorti de la bouche des *libres penseurs* ou des *esprits forts* du 18e siècle."

the same principles, whenever acted upon, will be found, almost invariably, to lead to the same consequences. Just such results as we see here brought about by the presumption of individual judgment and the rejection of authority again flowed from the unbridled outbreak of the same restive principles at the Reformation; heresy being, in both cases, the pioneer of infidelity, and the fancied triumphs of reason but ending, at last, in the death of all faith.

Having established two Gods, these Gnostic heretics could not be long in finding out that their system would be incomplete and inconsistent without having also two Saviours; —the attributes of the promised Messiah of the Jews being, according to their view, wholly different from those that characterized the Son and Messenger of the Supreme Father. The one had been announced as a conqueror, and as the restorer of the Jewish Empire, while the other came to bring peace and salvation to all people*. The Saviour of

* The Rabbins supposed, in the same manner, that there would be two Messiahs; the one poor, miserable,

the Demiurge was (according to the Creator's prophet, Isaiah,) to be called Emmanuel, which was not, said they, the name of Christ; and while the former had been promised as the Son of David, the latter altogether disclaimed the relationship. The solution which they gave of the whole difficulty was, that the real Saviour, unknown and unannounced as he had been to the world, was not unwilling to take advantage of the hope of a Messiah which the Prophets of the Creator had diffused among mankind, in order that by passing himself off as the Deliverer expected so long, he might the more effectually perform the great mission intrusted to him and emancipate this world from the yoke of the Demiurge. Leaving, therefore, the supreme Heavens of his Father, and traversing those of the Creator, he assumed, on approaching earth, the outward semblance of a man (without having recourse, said they, to the unworthy expedient of human

---

and devoted to death; the other, the restorer of the Jewish Empire. To Josephus, too, has been attributed the absurdity of believing that Christ was one Messiah and the Emperor Vespasian the other.

parentage and an incarnation) and made his appearance, for the first time, among men, in the synagogue of Capernaum, in the fifteenth year of the reign of Tiberius.

Entertaining notions so dark of the God of the Israelites, and of his Code, it was but consistent in these heretics to hold all connected with the Jewish Dispensation in the utmost horror. To such a length was this antipathy carried by them that the Marcionites, who made it a rule to fast on a Saturday, professed to do so from a mere feeling of spite to the Creator who had commanded the Jews to hold a feast on that day; and a branch of the Gnostics, called Antitactæ, did not hesitate to acknowledge that they infringed the commands of the Jewish God, solely because they were his.

But the sect which most systematically, and, considering the principle on which it was founded, most consistently followed up these views of the Old Testament, was that of the Ophites, or Serpentinians, by whom all persons who had, since the creation of the world, been known to have suffered for their opposition to the Creator's will, were regarded with affection and veneration as victims of an unjust God, and as martyrs to the hope of a better order of things under the Supreme Being and his son. Cain, for instance, was revered by them with peculiar fervour, and over the ruins of Sodom and Gomorrah they mourned most religiously. But the great object of their worship, and that from which they derived their name, was no other than the original Serpent himself, who, so far from being, as the world supposes, a tempter and deceiver, was, according to these dreamers, man's earliest and best benefactor. The command given to our first parents not to eat of the Tree of Knowledge was but a device, said they, planned by the jealous Jehovah to detach man from his protectress, the heavenly Sophia, and debar him from all knowledge of celestial things. That good Æon*, however,

---

* Among the titles given by the Valentinians to their Sophia was that of Κυριος, or Lord; and Tertullian ridi-

ever watchful over her charge, resolved to baffle the Creator, and sending Ophis, one of her Genii, in the form of a serpent, into Paradise, ordered him to persuade Adam to break this capricious law, and to eat of the fruit that would open to him all heavenly knowledge. According to some of the Ophites, too, this Serpent was no other than the Saviour himself,—as was manifest, they said, from the life-giving effects attributed to the brazen serpent in Numbers, xxi. 9, and the application of that type to Jesus, in John, iii. 14.

On the same principle, and with no less daring absurdity, did a branch of this sect single out Judas from all the Apostles of our Lord, as the only one sufficiently deep in the counsels of Heaven, to know of what infinite importance it was that Christ should be sacrificed by the Jews. Apprized secretly,

---

cules them with, perhaps, somewhat more facetiousness than beseems a grave Father of the Church, on the confusion which, in this, and in other instances, they fell into, respecting her sex:—" Ita," he says, " omnem illi honorem contulerunt fœminæ puto et barbam,—ne dixerim cætera."—*Adv. Valentin.*

said they, by the heavenly Sophia that the consequence of this death would be the downfall, for ever, of the Zabaoth, or Jewish God, he felt himself bound to accelerate so blessed a result, and thus, by betraying his Master, helped to save mankind*. For this insight into the true nature of the transaction they professed to be indebted to a Gospel written by Judas, which had descended to their sect, and was the only one, in their opinion, worthy of any credit†.

With respect to the ultimate result that was to arise out of all this complex agency

---

* These were also among the opinions held by the Cainites, or venerators of Cain, who proceeded exactly upon the same principle and, in most points, agreed with the Ophites. As all of these sects pretended to some special sources of information, the Cainites professed to have founded their peculiar tenets upon certain revelations made to them of those unutterable things which St. Paul had seen in his flight, or rapt, to the Third Heaven.

† The sect of the Ophites is said to have been in existence so late as the sixth century; and that they were numerous and flourishing in the time of Ephrem Syrus, appears highly probable from the pains taken by that Saint to denounce and curse them.

which the Gnostics supposed to be at work in the supernatural world, the consummation to which the Valentinians looked forward, as the crowning of the whole, was that finally all spiritual creatures shall be restored to their primitive nature, and, reaching at last the full maturity of perfection, shall ascend together into the Pleroma, there to dwell with the spiritual mates allotted to them, following, in this respect, the example of the Æon, Jesus himself, who shall then resume his high station in the celestial abode, linked for ever with his beatified bride, Sophia Achamoth*!

* In the Acts of the Apostle Thomas (one of the apocryphal books of the Encratitæ and other heretics,) we find an Ode expressly relating to this celestial marriage.

CHAPTER XXVI.

Catalogue of Heresies.—The Marcosians, Melchisedecians, Montanists, &c.—Why noticed.—Clemens Alexandrinus inclined to Gnosticism.—Tertullian, a Montanist.—St. Augustin, a Manichæan.

Having dwelt so long on these few branches of the luxuriant stem of Gnosticism, I have but little claim on the reader's patience for more than a hasty glance at some of the other forms of this and its kindred heresies; and the most compendious way, perhaps, will be to lay before him a short *catalogue raisonnée* of a few of the most remarkable of these sects that occur to me.*

* To those who are curious in the study of ancient heresies, I beg to recommend a work which, though compiled by a man of but little soundness of judgment, as regards his own opinions, is rich in information and references respecting the opinions of the heretics,—the *Elenchus Hæreticorum omnium* of Prateolus. For a more concise account of the different sects, Le Grand's *Historia Hæresiarcharum* may be consulted; and those who prefer seeing the subject treated in a Protestant sense, will find it ably done by the learned Ittigius, *De Hæresiarchis ævi Apostolici*, &c.

The Marcosians, as if to outdo the Trinity, established a sort of Quarternity in the Supreme Father, and maintained that the plenitude of Truth was to be found in the Greek alphabet*, grounding their fancy upon these words in the book of Revelation—" I am Alpha and Omega." Their founder, Mark, too, not only asserted that God had had several children, but spoke of these children (says St. Irenæus) with as much confidence as if he had been present at all their births.

The Melchisedecians, as their name imports, selected Melchisedec as the object of their

---

* Allowing his fancy to be carried away by a false notion of the Logos, or Word, the founder of the Marcosians supposed those emanations from the Deity which composed the heavenly Pleroma to have proceeded from him originally as *Words,* consisting each of a certain mystic number of letters. Thus the first word which the Supreme Being pronounced was a syllable of four letters, every one of which became a distinct being, and composed what Mark called the first Tetrad. The second word was also of four letters and formed the second Tetrad, completing that amount of spiritual entities to which the Valentinians gave the name of the Ogdoad. The third word was of ten letters, and so on,—through an infinite series of arithmetical and inconceivable nonsense.

worship, holding that he was a Dynamis, or divine power,—superior to Jesus Christ as being mediator between God and the Angels, whereas Christ was only mediator between God and Man.

The Messalians, having read in Scripture that " the Devil goes about like a roaring lion, seeking whom he may devour," and not content with a single prowler of this kind, imagined that the whole atmosphere was brimful of devils, and that people inhaled them with the vital air. In consequence of this idea, their whole time was passed in spitting and blowing their noses, in the intervals of which latter exercise, they imagined that they caught glimpses of the Trinity.

The Pereans, with a prodigality of divine means not very philosophical, established in their system three Fathers, three Sons, and three Holy Ghosts; and it is supposed to be against these sectaries that the Athanasians of the present day are called upon to protest when they say that " there is but one Father, not three Fathers; one Son, not three Sons; and one Holy Ghost, not three Holy Ghosts."

The Montanists, a most numerous and long flourishing sect, took it on the word of their founder that he was the very Paraclete promised by the Redeemer to perfect his new Law of the Gospel. These heretics (who are not to be accounted any branch of the Gnostics) held that God had already made two unsuccessful attempts to save mankind, first through the medium of Moses and the Prophets, and, secondly, by his own manifestation in the flesh. Both these plans, however, having failed, he was at last obliged to descend by the Holy Ghost, and divide himself, by a sort of triple inspiration, between Montanus and two ladies of quality, of no very reputable characters, who lived with him*. A particular branch of this sect, *the Ascites,* used to place near

---

* Prisca and Maximilla. Montanus boasted that to himself and his two Prophetesses had been given the fulness of God's spirit, whereas to St. Paul it had been but imperfectly communicated,—that Apostle himself having confessed, (1 Cor. xiii. 9) that he but " knew in part and prophesied in part."

their altar a kind of bladder, well blown up, and dance round it, regarding the bladder as an emblem of that spiritual inflation with which they themselves had been favoured by the Holy Ghost. Another branch, *the Tascodrugitæ*, or *Pattalorinchitæ*, made it a point of devotion to put their fingers upon their noses, or into their mouths, during prayer, professing therein, says St. Augustin, to imitate David;—" Set a watch, O Lord, before my mouth; keep the door of my lips*." (Ps. cxli. 3.)

The Manichees.—On the heresy of Manes, which began to flourish towards the end of the third century, the departing Spirit of Gnosticism seems to have let fall its dark mantle. In imitation of Christ, the founder of the Manichees professed to have been born of a virgin, and also attached to himself twelve apostles, by one of whom false Acts

---

* Another wise sect, the Discalceati, in order to show the accuracy of their spiritual knowledge, always went without shoes,—God having said to Moses (Exod. iii. 5) " Put off thy shoes from off thy feet."

were fabricated, and fathered on the Apostles of our Lord.

It may appear to some persons but an idle task thus to rake up such blasphemous follies; but, as showing the wantonness with which Private Judgment has, in so many instances, careered through Scripture, and the "fantastic tricks before high heaven" which, in these moods, it plays, such historical examples cannot be deemed unuseful. It should be recollected, too, that follies, however gross, become, when adopted by large portions of the human race, matters of grave import; and there is hardly one of the wild, senseless systems I have here enumerated that did not occupy the boasted reason of mankind, whether in supporting or refuting it, through a lapse of many centuries. The Gnostic sects had each their special Gospels, either forged, or corrupted from those of the Evangelists*;

---

* Thus the Ebionites made use of the Hebrew Gospel of St. Matthew, leaving out, however, as contrary to their belief in the simple humanity of Christ, the three first Chapters. Marcion composed a Gospel for himself by

and each also adopted a peculiar Canon of Scripture, rejecting (as did Luther afterwards, in the case of the Epistle of St. James,) whatever happened not to suit their respective purposes. The Marcionites, too, of whose wild system of Christianity I have just given some account, were able to boast not only martyrs, but a long succession of bishops.

Nor can we wonder that light, ordinary minds should have been whirled into these great Maelstroms of heresy, when, even among the Catholic Fathers themselves, some of the ablest were sucked into the vortex. In the Clementine Homilies, a work which though not of that high parentage its assumed name imports, seems acknowledged to have been the production of some eminent Christian of the second age, it is said of the Sophia of

mutilating and altering that of St. Luke;—and a question as to which was the most authentic, Marcion's Gospel or St. Luke's, has long been contested among the German Rationalists. The heretic, Tatian, instead of choosing, like the rest, some one of the four Evangelists, or some apocryphal relation, made a Code out of the four Gospels, which he called the Harmony of the Gospels.

the Gnostics, that God himself rejoices in her alliance. The language in which Clement of Alexandria speaks of the Gnosis breathes all the spirit of that sect*; and, so late as the beginning of the fifth century, we find in the Odes of the Bishop Synesius such a display of Gnostic thoughts and phrases as renders them far more like the compositions of a Valentinian or Marcosian than of a Catholic Pastor.

Of the catching influence of some of the other great heresies, we have yet more signal examples. The shrewd Tertullian was induced to believe in Montanus as the Paraclete promised by Christ, and, for a time, surrendered his strong mind to the gross delusions of that impostor and his two inspired women of quality. St. Augustin remained attached to the sect of the Manichees till his thirtieth year; and through him has the dark infection of this heresy been transmitted to succeeding

---

* The author of *L'Histoire du Gnosticisme* goes so far as to assert that, " Plus on examine les opinions des premiers siècles plus la Gnosis y apparait comme philosophie dominante."

ages,—even to the tinging of the sacred waters of Catholicity with its stain. A history, indeed, of the errors and extravagances of heresy * is but too closely connected with that of the human mind itself, as showing what derangement even the soundest intellects are exposed to by such extravasations of the life-blood of Faith out of those regular channels in which God designed it steadily and healthily to flow.

* How curiously, if not always usefully, an investigation of this kind may be made subservient to the illustration of the Sacred text itself, has been shown in those elaborate researches into the history of Gnosticism with which Dr. Burton has, in his Bampton Lecture, enriched the learned world.

In looking over this laborious work, I find a remark which I have hazarded some pages back, p. 249, (respecting the allusion contained in 1 Tim. iii. 20, to Gnosticism), anticipated and confirmed.

CHAPTER XXVII.

Discovery, at last, of Protestantism among the Gnostics.—Simon Magus the author of Calvinism.—Calvinistic doctrines held by the Valentinians, Basilidians, Manichæans, &c.

Though I may have been tempted, in the preceding chapters, by the curious nature of my subject, to indulge in somewhat more lengthened details, respecting the Gnostic sects, than the immediate purpose of these pages required, it must also, I think, have been observed that, in those apparently excursive inquiries, the main object of my pursuit has been seldom, if for an instant, forgotten. Nor, even thus far, had I any reason to complain of a want of success in my researches; since, as furnishing precedents for the free exercise of that great Protestant privilege which entitles every man to interpret the Scriptures according to his own judgment and fancy, the worthy believers in Sophia Achamoth had come up to the full pitch of all that my most independent tastes could desire. Promising, too, as all this looked, it was but the dawn of what I had yet to discover among these heretics. In taking thus such independent and self-willed views of Scripture, they but started on a principle common to all manner of heresies;—but I soon found that, as models for my purpose, their example did not stop here. In short, I discovered, to my great joy, that, in some of their leading doctrines, *the Gnostics were essentially and radically Protestant*.*

* I can answer confidently for my young friend that at the time when this discovery presented itself to him, he was not, in the least degree, aware that the late Bishop Tomline had, in his Refutation of Calvinism, put forth the same curious fact;—one of the Chapters of the Bishop's work being entitled as follows, " Opinions of earliest Heretics bearing resemblance to Calvinism."

The fact, however, of Calvinism being but a reproduction of the Gnostic, and other heresies, is too obvious not to have struck learned observers, long before the time of Bishop Tomline. The illustrious Dutch divine, Lindanus, in his Dialogues on the revival of ancient heresies, enforced ably and incontrovertibly the same

My readers, no doubt, will remember the exceeding joy and surprise with which, at the close of my long search after Protestantism in the first ages, I at length stumbled on a stanch Calvinist in the person of Simon Magus. "*Not by virtuous actions* (said this heretic) *but by Grace is salvation to be attained.*" It will also, perhaps, be recollected that, from certain generous scruples, I then hesitated to take advantage of such disreputable authority; and, though long foreseeing that my Protestantism must be of heretical descent, yet felt anxious, for the honour of all parties, that it should be of some better breed. To say the truth, too, I was not quite sure that this glimpse of genuine Calvinism might not be, after all, but a chance sparkle, and that I should see nothing more of it. On passing on, however, from the Arch-heretic to the numerous sects that sprung from him, I found this feature of the parent faithfully repro-

point; and by the celebrated scholar, Petavius, in the Preface prefixed by him to the works of Epiphanius, it is no less strongly asserted.

duced in all his offspring; I found that they all, in some point or other, anticipated the Reformed lights of Geneva and Wittemburgh; and that if I had, at once, designated Simon Magus as the fount and wellspring of some of the most boasted of the Protestant doctrines, I should have asserted no more than it was now in my power indisputably to prove.

The utter depravity of Man's nature,—the insufficiency, or rather nullity of good works towards salvation,—the powerlessness of the human will,—the doctrines of election, reprobation, and perseverance,—such are the great points of what is now called "Vital Christianity" on which I found the very spirit of the Reformation reigning throughout these sects; and could I have been content to receive my Protestantism at the hands of Christians who believed in two Gods, two Saviours, and a maternal Holy Ghost, I might from these Evangelical repositories have provided myself to my heart's content.

In each of the Gnostic sects, for instance, there was a distinct class of persons, who alone were thought sufficiently spiritual to be certain of salvation, while all others were considered reprobate and incapable of saving themselves. These chosen few the Valentinians called the *Elect Seed,* holding that their faith did not come by instruction, but by nature and election. " They affirm," says Irenæus, " that they themselves shall be entirely and completely saved, not by their own conduct, but because they are spiritual by nature*."

The same doctrine of Election was maintained also by Basilides,—coupled with that other Calvinistic doctrine which necessarily results from it, the slavery of the human will:—" He tells us (says St. Clement of Alexandria) that faith is not the rational consent of a mind endowed with free-will. The precepts then, both of the Old and New Testament are superfluous, if any one be saved by nature, as Valentinus maintains, and if any one be faithful and elect by nature, as Basilides thinks." By another also of these

---

* Αυτους δε μη δια πραξεως αλλα δια το φυσει πνευματικους ειναι παντη τε και παντως δογματιζουσιν σωθησεσθαι.—*Iren.*

heresiarchs, Bardesanes, it was, in like manner, asserted, that man can do nothing of himself, being a creature wholly without freedom, and impelled by irresistible decrees*.

The high Calvinistic tenets of the inamissibility of Grace and the Perseverance of the Elect were maintained as resolutely by the Valentinians as by the Synod of Dort itself†. "Gold," said they, "though fallen in the mire, is still gold, and loses nothing of its original lustre or nature. Even so is it with

---

* In the accounts given of the opinions of this heretic there is some apparent inconsistency. Though he was the author (as we know from Eusebius) of a work against Destiny, he is yet represented as having been an advocate for the doctrine of fatality. The truth seems to be that he considered *souls* as exempt from the laws of destiny, but looked upon all connected with *bodies* as under the control of fate and the stars.

† "Such as have once received that grace by faith can never fall from it finally or totally, notwithstanding the most enormous sins they can commit."—*Synod of Dort*, *Art.* 5. Even the canting phraseology of our modern Saints is manifestly derived from the same source. Thus, St. Justin tells us of some of these Elect persons who said of themselves that "though they were sinners, yet if they *knew* God, the Lord would not impute to them sin."

the Elect;—let their conduct be what it may, they can never forfeit their high distinctive privilege."—(*Irenæus.*) The natural consequences of such dangerous doctrine showed themselves then, as on its revival, at the Reformation. " Wherefore," says the same writer, " those of them who are the most perfect do without fear all things which are forbidden." " I speak," says Clement of Alexandria, " of the followers of Basilides, who lead incorrect lives, as persons authorized to sin because of their perfection*; or who will certainly be saved by nature, even though they sin now, because of an election founded in nature."

The Manichæans, from whom more directly was transmitted to our heretics the gloomy doctrine of the utter depravity of man, held

---

* Some of these sects, not unworthy forerunners of the Anabaptists, declared that a community of goods and of wives was the just and true happiness of their Elect:— Ἡ πασων ουσιων και γυναικων πηγη της θειας εστι δικαιοσυνης :— which words form the commencement of one of those curious Inscriptions, said to have been found near Cyrene, and first published by the learned Rationalist, Gesenius.

also many of the other precious tenets that have descended with this bequest. " Manichæus asserts (says St. Jerom) that his Elect are free from all sin, and that they could not sin if they would." The same Father says, " Let us briefly reply to those slanderers who reproach us, by saying that it belongs to the Manichæans to condemn the nature of man and to take away free-will."

Here, then, had I, at last, accomplished the discovery, not only of a single sect, but of whole tribes and generations of Protestants;—a discovery as unlooked for, and certainly far more authentic than that of the snug nest of Presbyterians, which Ledwich found out among the wilds of Tipperary, in the middle of the sixth century*. Could I have detected but a millesimal part of this high Protestantism among the *orthodox* of the first ages, how my heart would have rejoiced! how my conscience would have been soothed by the discovery! One particle, one drop of such true Geneva

---

* The Culdees.

doctrine would have sent me to my pillow in comfort. But, no—base, indeed, was the resource to which I now found myself reduced; and accordingly, urgent as were my motives for conversion, I came sturdily to the resolution that, rather than exchange the bright, golden armour of the old Catholic Saints for this heretical brass, lackered over by modern hands, I would submit to the worst doom my worldly fate could have in store for me.

CHAPTER XXVIII.

Another search for Protestantism among the orthodox as unsuccessful as the former.—Fathers the very reverse of Calvinists.—Proofs.—St. Ignatius, St. Justin, &c.—Acknowledged by Protestants themselves.

ON returning again to the train of thought which had thus occupied me, and reflecting how lucky I should have accounted myself, could I have detected, among the orthodox of the Primitive Church, any such specimens of Protestantism as I was here furnished with by the Gnostics, I could not help asking myself, with some anxiety, *was* I, after all, so sure that no such specimens could be found? *had* I, in fact, sufficiently examined into the dogmas of the early Church to have been fully satisfied that no such opinions as I have been detailing were among them; or *could* it, indeed, be possible that the doctrines of election and reprobation, of the inefficacy of good works towards salvation, the slavery of the human will, the utter inability of man to do the will of God,—that all these doctrines, now dignified with the name of "vital Christianity," so far from being sanctioned by the authority of the early lights of the Church*, are to be found only in the distempered dreams of those heretical sects against which the Church had, from the first dawn of her existence, to combat?

Such were now the questions I put to myself, and, strange to say, unsuccessful as I had hitherto been in all my exploratory journeys into the region of orthodoxy, a last, feeble hope sprung up, that possibly, on a little further search, I might discover that the Gnostic heretics had not kept all the Calvinism to themselves, but that some foretaste of this sour fruit was to be found also among the Fathers. Seldom, I will do myself the justice to say, has any instance occurred of a

---

* " What is that to us of the Church (says Origen) who condemn those who maintain, that there are some persons formed by nature to be saved, and others formed by nature to perish."—*Contr. Cels.*

chase followed up, through all reverses, with such unbaffled ardour;—but, alas, this new hope was as fallacious as any of its predecessors. Instead of finding, in the works of the Fathers, the least shadow of a sanction for the horrible * notion, assumed alike by

---

* The very epithet which Calvin himself applies to his doctrine of Reprobation:—" Decretum *horribile* fateor." " Is it not wonderful (says Bishop Tomline) that any one should ascribe to the God of all mercy a Decree which he himself confesses to be horrible?"

That the weapons of most modern heresies are but those of the old ones refurbished, is a remark which has been more than once suggested in these pages; and, as an illustration of it, we may observe that the very same texts now relied upon by the Calvinists, for the support of their favourite doctrines of election and reprobation, were those referred to, for the very same purpose, by their predecessors, the Gnostics, no less than sixteen or seventeen hundred years ago. After quoting several of these texts (Gal. i. 15, 16; Rom. i. 1; Jerem. i. 5; Ps. li. 5, xxii. 10, lviii. 3.) St. Jerom says, " The Heretics who pretend that there are different natures, and that the one is saved and that the other perishes, maintain from these passages that no one would be understood to be just before he did some good, or would be hated as a sinner before some crime was committed, unless there was a different nature of those who perish and of those who are to be saved."

Gnostics and Calvinists, that a select portion of mankind has been singled out for salvation, while all the rest of the human race has been created but to be damned, I read in those authorised expounders of our Faith the very reverse of all this. I found in the excellent St. Justin the far different assurance that the seeds of the Divine Word are implanted equally in all men, and that all who have the will to obtain mercy from God are gifted also with the power.

Still earlier did I read in the apostolic St. Ignatius that "if any one be pious, he is a man of God; but if any one be impious, he is a man of the Devil, *being made so, not by nature, but by his own will.*" Instead of the picture drawn of human nature by Bardesanes and Calvin, who describe man as a chained slave of destiny, without power or free-will, I saw him represented in the pages of these same Fathers, a free, responsible agent, endowed with a self-determining power towards good or ill*, and having eternal happiness or

* " He (St. Justin) speaks of a self-determining power in man (αυτεξουσιον) and uses much the same kind of rea-

misery dependent on his choice. " I find that man (says Tertullian) was formed by God with free-will, and with power over himself, observing in him no image or likeness to God more than in this respect. . . . . . The law also itself, which was then imposed by God, confirmed this condition of man. For a law would not have been imposed on a person who had not in his power the obedience due to the law; nor would transgression have been threatened with death, if the contempt also of the law were not placed to the account of his free-will."

Again, instead of depreciating,—as Simon Magus and, after him, Luther and Cavin have done,—the efficacy of Good Works, thus triumphantly did I find a contemporary of the apostles extolling their high value. " Let us hasten with cheerfulness and alacrity to perform every good work. . . . . Let us observe that all just men have been adorned with good

soning on the obscure subject of free-will as has been fashionable with many since the days of Arminius."—*Milner's History of the Church.*

works. And even the Lord himself, having adorned himself with good works, rejoiced. Having therefore his example, let us fulfil his will; let us work the work of righteousness with all our strength. We must ever be ready in well-doing: for from thence all things are derived."—*S. Clement.*

But it is unnecessary to refer any further to the numerous citations I had collected to prove that, in none of the Fathers of the Church, before the time of St. Augustin, is any trace of those Protestant doctrines, now called Evangelical, to be found*; but that, on the contrary, while Simon Magus and his followers were engendering that dark brood of fancies which, in later ages, were to be again quickened into life by Calvin and Luther, the Catholic Church was, through the tongues of her great orators and teachers, asserting eloquently the Universality of the

---

* From a passage in the Institutes (Lib. ii. c. 5. sect. 15.) it is evident that Calvin himself considered Augustin to be the only one of all the ancient Fathers that could be cited as favourable to his doctrine.

Redemption by Christ, the Freedom of the Human Will*, the precious efficacy of Good Works and Repentance, and the ability of every Christian to work out his salvation. It is unnecessary, I repeat, to take any pains to prove this fact, as already a host of Protestant divines, of all schools of divinity, have conceded it.

The Lutheran, Flacius, for instance, accuses those Fathers, who wrote soon after the Apostles, of being totally ignorant of man's natural corruption, and other such mysteries since discovered in the Gospel†; while the Calvinist, Milner, pretending to find, in the first century, some glimpses of his own doctrines, confesses that, after that

---

* "The Soul is endowed with free-will (says Origen) and is at liberty to incline either way." To prove that "man has a free-will to believe or not to believe," St. Cyprian quotes Deuteronomy (xxx. 19): "I have set before you life and death, blessing and cursing; therefore choose life, that thou and thy seed may live."

† In the same manner Basnage, too, complains *(Hist. des Eglises Ref.)* that the ancient Christians expressed themselves "maigrement" on these subjects.

period, these evangelical truths faded away, and were by almost all the succeeding Fathers denied or forgotten. Of Irenæus and St. Justin, who wrote in the second century, he says:—" They are silent, or nearly so, on the Election of Grace; and defend the Arminian notion of Free-will." After taxing St. Clement of Alexandria with a similar want of vital Christianity, he thus (with the arrogance so hereditarily characteristic of a sect of which Simon Magus, the self-constituted rival of Christ, was the parent), cavalierly dismisses that learned Father:— " On the whole, this writer, learned, laborious, and ingenious as he was, may seem to be far exceeded by many obscure and illiterate persons at this day in true scriptural knowledge and in the experience of divine things."

Well might the judicious Lardner, in noticing some similar instance of presumptuous judgment upon the Fathers, with happy irony, exclaim,—" Poor ignorant Primitive Christians, I wonder how they could find the way to heaven. They lived near the times of

Christ and his Apostles. They highly valued and diligently read the Holy Scriptures, and some of them wrote Commentaries upon them; but yet it seems they knew little or nothing of their religion, though they embraced and professed it with the manifest hazard of all earthly good things, and many of them laid down their lives rather than renounce it. Truly, we of these times are very happy in our orthodoxy; but I wish that we did more excel in the virtues which they and the Scriptures likewise, I think, recommend as the distinguishing properties of a Christian."

CHAPTER XXIX.

Return to Heretics.—Find Protestantism in abundance.—Novatians, Agnoetæ, Donatists, &c.—Aerius, the first Presbyterian.—Accusations of Idolatry against the Catholics.—Brought forward by the Pagans, as now by the Protestants.—Conclusion of the Volume.

I HAD now taken my last, positively last, trip into the old orthodox world in quest of Protestantism; and weary as I was of so fruitless, so wild-goose a chase, it was with an ill zest I again returned to the study of my heretics, of whom I now began to be as much ashamed as Falstaff was of his regiment. Having imposed upon myself, however, the task of tracing Heresy through the Four first Ages, I was resolved to go through with my work; and the same run of good luck in finding Protestants,—if good luck it could be called to find them where I did not want them,—among the heterodox and schismatic, still continued to attend me. Far less amusing, however, were these later acquaintances than my old Calvinist friends, the believers in Sophia Achamoth; and, whatever indulgence I might have been inclined to feel towards Private Judgment, in her skittish moods, I now found that to be dull, as well as heterodox, is a sort of supererogation not to be tolerated. I shall content, therefore, myself with singling out, from the heresies of this period, a few of those which, from their peculiarly Anti-Catholic doctrines, may be regarded as the chief channels through which the elements of Protestantism have been transmitted, in full Gnostic perfection, to modern times.

And first, to begin with the Novatians:— these sectaries, who flourished about the middle of the third century, and whose founder is described by St. Cyprian as "a deserter from the Church, a teacher of pride, and a corrupter of the truth," were nevertheless, in their way, as good Protestants as need be, seeing that they denied stoutly to the Church the power of absolving penitent sinners, refused peremptorily to acquiesce in her authority and traditions, and made their appeal, as all other heretics have done, before and since, to Reason. The language, indeed, of St. Pacian*, in addressing one of these sectaries, may, with the simple substitution of the words placed between brackets, be applied with equal point by a Catholic of the present day to Protestants.

" Who was it (he asks) that proposed this doctrine? was it Moses, or Paul, or Christ? No; it was Novatian [Luther]. And who was he? was he a man pure and blameless, who had been lawfully ordained Bishop? . . . . . And what of all this, you will tell me;—it suffices that he has thus taught. But when did

---

* Of this writer, who flourished in the fourth century, Mr. Clarke *(Succession of Ecclesiastical Literature)* pronounces that he "was no less pious than eloquent;" adding, that " there are more errors of the Romish church, supported in a bolder way and with more direct evidence, in this Father, than perhaps in any other of double the bulk." With all these " blushing" errors " thick upon him," how comes it, let me ask, that St. Pacian was not considered as an *innovator* by his contemporaries, but, on the contrary, had the reputation of being one of the most acute and orthodox divines of his day? The solution is not difficult.

he thus teach? was it immediately after the passion of Christ? No; it was nearly three hundred [sixteen hundred] years after that event. But did this man follow the Prophets? was he a prophet? did he raise the dead? did he work miracles? did he speak various tongues? for to establish a new Gospel he should have done some of these things." The Saint then stating explicitly the Protestant principle upon which these heretics proceeded, "You say, *we do not acquiesce in authority; we make use of reason,*" adds, "As to myself, who have been hitherto *satisfied with the authority and tradition of the Church,* I will not now dissent from it."

Our next sample of good Protestantism is found among the Eunomians, a branch of the Arian heresy, and infected, as was Arius himself, with Gnosticism. The founder of this sect held also, with Valentinian, Basilides, &c., the convenient doctrine of the Perseverance of the Elect, maintaining that all who embraced the truth (meaning thereby *his* opinions) would never fall from a state of grace. Among these, saving opinions the principal was, that Christ is *not* consubstantial with the Father*. This excellent Protestant opposed himself also to the old Catholic practice of paying reverence to relics, and invoking the intercession of Saints; calling, as St. Jerom tells us, by the facetious name of " Antiquarians," all those who attached any value to the bones and relics of Martyrs.

The Agnoetæ, or Ignorants (as from their peculiar opinion they were called), afford another strong example of that sort of heirloom of error which heretics transmit to their successors, from age to age;—our Saviour's professed ignorance of the time of the Day of Judgment (Mark, xiii. 32) on which these sectaries founded their cavils against his God-

---

* The shrewd argument, as Cave pronounces it, by which Eunomius supported this position is as follows:— a simple Essence, such as is the Divine Being, cannot contain within itself two principles of which one is begetting and the other begot; or, (as I take to have been his meaning, in somewhat plainer terms). a simple Being, like God, cannot be at once the Begetter and the Begotten.

head*, having also furnished to that large class of Protestants, called Unitarians, one of the most plausible arguments for their still more extensive unbelief. And such is the cycle which errors seem ever destined to perform, —vanishing away, from time to time, and then darkly reappearing. The very same arms with which the detracters of Christ's divinity

---

* Among those texts which the dangerous ingenuity of Private Judgment has contrived to wrest into evidence against the Divinity of the Saviour, this referred to by the Agnoetæ seems to have been found by the Fathers the most difficult to unravel. Some answered that the Son of God meant only that he had no experimental knowledge of the matter. St. Augustin endeavours to get rid of the difficulty by the very forced explanation that by *not knowing*, in this passage, is meant his not making others to know. Some more modern theologians have contented themselves with the very simple solution that "when Christ told his apostles he did not know on what day precisely the general judgment would take place, he very possibly did not give any actual attention to the circumstance."— *(Forbes, Inst. Theolog. l. 3, c. 21.)* The distinction of the two natures, established by the Council of Chalcedon, affords the only explanation of this and other such difficulties. While as *God*, Christ knew all things; there was much of which, as *Man*, he may be supposed to have been ignorant.

assailed the Catholic Doctors of other times, are but again furbished up by the Priestleys and Belshams against the Trinitarian Divines of our own.

The sect of the Donatists, which may be accounted rather a schism than a heresy, and which laid claim to exclusive orthodoxy for Donatist Churches,—saying that "God was in Africa, and *not* elsewhere,"—have in so far a claim to be mentioned honourably in Protestant annals that they were the first Christians, I believe, who conferred upon the Catholic Church the polite title of " Whore of Babylon."

We next come to a worthy precursor of the Presbyterians, Aerius, who, having in vain tried to be appointed a Bishop himself, took his revenge by making war on all Bishops whatsoever[*], declaring that they had no right to

---

[*] In disappointed ambition may most frequently be found the source of those movements by which restless spirits have agitated mankind. Thus Marcion became a heretic on being denied Church preferment; and, with the same feeling, Vanini wrote to the Pope that, if his Holiness did not give him a benefice, he would, in twelve months from that time, overturn the Christian religion.

any superiority or jurisdiction over Presbyters. This early champion of the Kirk opposed also the Catholic practice of praying for the dead, and denied to the Church the power of instituting Fasts, saying that every one had a right to choose his own time of fasting. In the reason given by him for this latter claim of independence, namely, that it might be thus shown we were no longer living under the Law, but under Grace, may be observed the workings of that same antipathy to the Law and its precepts, which has been transmitted, through a regular succession of heretics, from the Christian Gnostics down to our modern Antinomians. My chief motive, however, for referring to the sect of the Aerians has been for the sake of the valuable testimony which their heresy affords to the antiquity of the solemn Catholic rite of prayers for the dead,—their dissent from which, in the middle of the fourth century, could never have drawn upon them, so decisively and generally, the brand of heresy, had not this practice descended to those times hallowed by ancient recollections, and sanctioned by the traditions of the Primitive Church.

The same remark will be found applicable to some of the doctrines of Vigilantius, who, though belonging properly to the commencement of the Fifth Century, may be allowed as a single exception to the rule I have imposed upon myself of not extending these researches beyond the close of the Fourth. This heretic, who holds a high rank among the Protoplasts of Protestantism, was a writer of what, in the present day, would be called smart anti-popery pamphlets,—laughing, with some degree of humour, at the reverence paid by Catholics to Relics, and at the prayers of Invocation which they addressed to their Saints. " They light up," says he, " large tapers at mid-day, and proceed to kiss and *adore* a small handful of dust. It must, no doubt, be a mighty service to the Martyrs thus to light up a few bad candles for those whom the Lamb, seated upon his throne, illuminates with all the splendour of his majesty*."

* In his answer to Vigilantius St. Jerom says—" The

We may here see how far from modern is the disingenuous trick of charging Catholics with being *adorers* of Relics and Images, in the very teeth of their own repeated disclaimers of such idolatry. The flat denial given by St. Jerom to the ribald charge of Vigilantius was, no doubt, as little listened to by the followers of that heretic as are similar declarations of the Catholics of our own days by the implicit readers of the lucubrations of the Rev. G. S. Faber and Co.—"We do *not* worship," says the Saint, "we do *not* adore either the relics of Martyrs, or Angels, or Cherubim, or Seraphim,—lest we serve the creature rather than the Creator, who is blessed for evermore. But we honour the relics of the Martyrs, that our minds may be raised to *Him* whose Martyrs they are. We honour them, that this honour may be referred to Him who says 'He that receiveth you, receiveth me' (Matt. x. 40)." Again,

Bishop of Rome, then, does wrong, in offering sacrifice to God over the venerable bones of those dead men Paul and Peter (according to you, but vile dust), and in regarding the tombs of those Saints as altars."

he exclaims indignantly, " Thou madman! who ever yet *adored* the Martyrs? who ever yet fancied that a mortal was a God?"

But this unfair policy of the adversaries of the Catholics is of a still more ancient date than even the times of St. Jerom; and, like almost every other point in the relative position of the two parties, may be traced back as far as the Apostolic age. Even then was the same spirit of misrepresentation alive; even then was the homage offered to the enshrined relics of an Ignatius or a Polycarp denounced by scoffers at the Faith as being an idolatrous transfer of that worship to the creature which belongs only to the Creator. That this was the case, in the instance of Polycarp, appears by a Letter from the Church of Smyrna, of which he was Bishop, giving to the Faithful an account of all the circumstances of his martyrdom. " It was suggested," say they, " that we would desert our crucified Master and begin to worship Polycarp. Foolish men! who know not that we can never desert Christ, who died for the salvation of all men, nor worship any other. Him we adore as the Son of God; but we show deserved respect to the Martyrs, as his disciples and followers. The Centurion, therefore, caused the body to be burnt. We then gathered his bones, more precious than pearls and more tried than gold, and buried them. In this place, God willing, we will meet and celebrate with joy and gladness the birthday of his Martyr, as well in memory of those who have been crowned before, as by his example to prepare and strengthen others for the combat."—*Euseb. Hist. Eccles. l.* 4, *c.* 15.

Thus it is, as I have already observed, that the relative position of the two parties, —the Catholic Church on one side, and the protesters against her doctrine on the other, —has been, from the first, and through all ages, virtually the same; the old truths remaining still unchanged, and the old errors, like often detected delinquents, reappearing again and again, under other names, so that, in fact, the Calvinism, Antinomianism, &c. of modern times are little else than *aliases* of the Gnosticism and Manichæism of times past.

Still more evident might this remarkable fact be made to appear by a yet further inquiry into the history of past heresies; but I have already sufficiently tried my reader's patience on this subject. Enough too has, perhaps, been said to show what fantastic gambols the various and ever-teeming spawn of Heresy have, at all times, played around the venerable ark of the Church in her majestic navigation through the great Deep of Ages;—while in vain attempting to sully or perplex her path, shoal after shoal of these monsters have descended into darkness, leaving the one, bright, buoyant Refuge of the Faithful to pursue unharmed, to the end of time, her Saving way.

NOTES.

Page 23.

Irenæus, in citing the Shepherd, calls it " Scripture," from which some have concluded that he really held it to be Canonical:—" illud etiam non omittendum quod Hermæ Pastorem velut canonicam Scripturam laudet Irenæus." (*Massuet Dissert. Præv. in Iren.*) Lardner, however, has shown that Irenæus uses the word here merely as a " writing " or " book."

St. Clement of Alexandria, no less than Origen, seems to have considered the Shepherd as a divinely inspired work.—Θειως τοινυν ἡ δυναμις ἡ τω Ερμᾶ κατα αποκαλυψιν λαλουσα.—*Strom. Lib.* 1.

Page 26.

So strict a faster was St. Ambrose that he never dined, we are told, but on Saturdays, on Lord's Days, and the Festivals of Martyrs. It is said that Monica, St. Augustin's mother, was greatly offended, on her coming to Milan, to find Ambrose dining on the Saturday; having observed that day to be kept as a solemn fast at Rome, and in other places, and therefore wondering that it should be held as a festival at Milan.

Page 33.

"*The Real Presence,*" &c.

It is hardly necessary to say that whenever in these pages, I make use of the phrase Real Presence, I mean to include also the necessary consequence of that miracle, Transubstantiation. Once the corporal Presence is admitted, the change of the substance of the sacramental elements follows as a matter of course. It has been always the policy, however, of Protestants, and for very evident reasons, to direct their attacks solely against the absurd process, as they choose to term it, of Transubstantiation; which is about as shallow and unfair a way of arguing as it would be to assume the mere *numerical* difficulty attendant on the doctrine of the Trinity as the sole grounds for objecting to it.

In the disputations between Catholics and Protestants in the reign of Edward VI., the latter invariably took this unfair vantage ground; the Catholics anxiously, but vainly, endeavouring to have the question of the Real Presence settled, in its natural order, previously to the discussion of the question of Transubstantiation. Both the motives and the futility of this subterfuge have been thus well exposed by Bossuet:—" Pour conserver dans les cœurs des peuples la haine du dogme Catholique il a fallu la tourner contre un autre objet que la Présence Réelle. La Transubstantiation est maintenant le grand crime: *ce n'est plus rien de mettre Jésus Christ présent; de mettre tout un corps dans chaque pareille; le grand crime est d'avoir oté le pain: ce qui regarde Jésus Christ est peu de chose; ce qui regarde le pain est essentielle.*"

Page 41.

" I am so far from being ashamed," says St. Augustine, " of the Cross, that I do not put the Cross of Christ in some hidden place, but carry it on my forehead."

Page 44.

The employment of the fish as a symbol of the name of Christ arose from the word ιχθυς being composed of the initial letters of the words Ιησους Χριστος, Θεου υιος, Σωτηρ. In the spurious Sibylline verses there are some acrostics beginning with these letters. For the same reason, as well as no doubt from their use of the rite of Baptism, Christians themselves were, in the first ages, called Fishes. " Sed nos Pisciculi (says Tertullian) secundum ιχθυν, secundum nostrum Jesum Christum in aquâ noscimur."

Page 47.

" *On the subject of exclusive salvation as Catholic as need be.*"

This is also the language, however, of the Protestant Church. " The visible Church consists of all those throughout the world who profess the true religion, out of which there is no ordinary possibility of salvation." (*Westminster Confession, ratified by Parliament, A. D. 1649.*) " Christ," says Bishop Pearson, " never appointed two roads to heaven, nor did he build a Church to save some, and another for other men's salvation. As none, then, were saved in the Deluge, but those who were within the ark of Noah, so none shall ever escape the eternal wrath of God, who belong not to the Church of God."— *Exposition of the Creed.*

In cases of invincible ignorance or invincible necessity, the Catholic Church admits of exceptions to this sweeping sentence. Thus, in the *Censure* passed by the Sorbonne on Rousseau's Emile, we find it laid down:—
"Tout homme qui est dans l'ignorance invincible des verités de la Foi ne sera jamais puni de Dieu pour n'avoir pas crû ces vérités. Telle est la doctrine Chrétienne et Catholique (*Art.* 26)—Quant aux communions separées de l'Eglise, les enfants et les simples qui vivent dans ces communions ne participent ni à la hérésie ni au schisme ; ils en sont excusés par leur ignorance invincible de l'état des choses. Il n'est pas du tout impossible à ceux qui vivent dans des communions separées de l'Eglise Catholique de parvenir, autant qu'il est nécessaire pour leur salut à la connaissance de la révélation Chrétienne (*art.* 32)."

The eminent Catholic Prelate, Frayssinous, thus asserts the same reasonable and charitable doctrine : "L'ignorance involontaire de la révélation n'est pas une faute punissable . . . . La révélation Chrétienne est une loi positive, et il est de la nature d'une loi de n'être obligatoire que lorsqu'elle est publiée et connue."—*Conférences.*

Page 68.

"*The injudicious excess of zeal which led Bonaventura,*" &c.

The Psaltery of Bonaventura is one of those monuments of extravagant zeal which, though constantly condemned by Catholics themselves, will as constantly be taken advantage of by their enemies, for the purpose of casting imputations on them. The late Mr. Charles Butler, in replying to the attacks of Mr. Southey and Dr. Philpotts, as well on the subject of this Psaltery, as of the Catholic hymn, *Impera Redemptori*, does not seem to have been aware that Grotius had to perform the same task before him. In reference to a work written by one James Laurence, this great man, writing to his brother, says, " In defiance of all justice, he charges the Psaltery of Bonaventura upon the whole body of Catholics (though it was condemned by the Doctors of the Sorbonne), and those verses to the Virgin Mary which commence with *Impera Redemptori*, as well as some others which he has quoted from their books."

In the same letter, with his usual enlightened candour, Grotius does justice to the views of the Catholics, on other essential points of their faith. " It is also possible," he says, " for persons in that Communion to avoid idolatry, by honouring the Saints only as the servants of God, by using images as refreshing excitements to their memories, and by venerating in the Sacrament that which is its principal part; as the Council of Trent has made the Adoration of the Sacrament to be tantamount to adoring Christ in the Sacrament." For an account of the efforts made ineffectually by Grotius to inspire with a portion of his own enlarged and conciliatory spirit the contending parties of his day, the reader will do well to consult *Nicholls's Arminianism and Calvinism compared*,—a work full of interesting reflection and research.

Page 73.

With a like view of the subject, Dr. Johnson says, that " the generality of mankind are neither so obstinately wicked as to deserve everlasting punishment, nor so good as to merit being admitted into the society of celestial spirits, and that God is therefore generously pleased to allow a middle state, where they may be purified by a certain degree of suffering."

These testimonies of Paley and Johnson to the Catholic doctrine of Purgatory suggest to me to lay before the reader a few other such candid admissions, on the part of Protestants, of the truth of our Catholic tenets, which I shall here class under their respective heads, referring for further examples to the Second Volume of this work, Chap. V.

PROTESTANT TESTIMONIES IN FAVOUR OF CATHOLIC DOCTRINES.

Primacy of the Pope.

The canonical grounds of the Primacy, as well as the necessity of such a jurisdiction for the preservation of unity, are thus strongly asserted by Grotius:—

" Restitutionem Christianorum in unum idemque corpus semper optatum à Grotio sciunt qui eum nôrunt. Existimavit autem aliquando incipi à Protestantium inter se conjunctione. Postea vidit id planè fieri nequire; quia præterquam quod Calvinistorum ingenia fermè omnium ab omni pace sunt alienissima, Protestantes nullo inter se Communi Ecclesiastico regimine sociantur. Quæ causæ sunt cur facile partes in unum Protestantium Corpus colligi nequeant; immo et cur partes aliæ atque aliæ sunt exsurrecturæ. Quare nunc planè sentit Grotius, et multi cum ipso, non posse Protestantes inter se jungi nisi simul jungantur cum iis qui Sedi Romanæ cohærent, sine quâ nullum sperari potest in Ecclesia Commune Regimen. Ideo optat ut ea divulsio quæ evenit et causæ divulsionis tollantur. *Inter eas causas non est Primatus*

Episcopi Romani, secundum Canones, fatente Melancthone, qui eum Primatum etiam necessarium putat ad retinendam Unitatem."—*Last Reply to Rivetus, Apol. Discuss.*

Grotius had held nearly the same language, with respect to what he calls " the *force* of the Primacy," in his first Reply to Rivetus:—" Quæ verò est causa cur qui opinionibus dissident inter Catholicos, maneant eodem corpore non ruptâ communione: contra, qui inter Protestantes dissident idem facere nequeant, utcumque multa de dilectione Fraterna loquantur? Hoc qui rectè expendent invenient *quanta sit vis Primatus.*"—*Ad Art.* 7.

" Whosoever reads their writings will find those of the fourth and fifth ages giving the supremacy to the Bishop of Rome, and asserting, that to him belongs the care of all Churches."—*Dumoulin, Vocation of Pastors.*

" Rome being a Church consecrated by the residence of St. Peter, whom antiquity acknowledged as the Head of the Apostolic Church, might easily have been considered, by the Council of Chalcedon, as the Head of the Church."—*Blondel on the Supremacy.*

In the course of some observations on the subject of the Papal Power and its advantages during the middle ages, Daines Barrington says, " There was a great use to Europe in general from there being a common referee in all national controversies, who could not himself ever think of extending his dominions, though he might often make a most improper use of his power as a mediator." He adds, " The ancients seem to have found the same convenience, in referring their disputes to the Oracle at Delphi."—*Observations on the ancient Statutes.*

After acknowledging the uncertainty of the Scriptures as a rule of faith, a living writer, Dr. Arnold, continues thus:—" Aware of this state of things, and aware also, with characteristic wisdom, of the deadly evil of religious divisions, the Roman Catholic Church ascribed to the sovereign power in the Christian society, in every successive age, an infallible spirit of truth, whereby the real meaning of any disputed passage of Scripture might be certainly and authoritatively declared; and if the Scripture were silent, then the living voice of the Church might supply its place; and being guided by the same Spirit which had inspired the Written Word, might pronounce upon any new point of controversy with a decision of no less authority."—*Principles of Church Reform.*

Penance, Confession, &c.

" Even the long and tedious penances which were of old enjoined to excommunicated persons, were only proofs of the faithful tenderness of the primitive pastors towards the souls of their people. Divines, of late years, have laboured to prove that Repentance imports nothing but an act of the mind; and 'tis true, that the repentance which fits grown men for baptism, does imply no more than a mere change of our resolution . . . . . but that repentance which is required of Christians, who, fallen from grace, and run into habits of vice or acts of very grievous sin, is of another sort, and was believed by the Guides and Fathers of the Apostolic age to import outward austerities, frequent fastings, and a long course of humiliation, in public as well as in private, as they sufficiently showed by their constant practice. . . . . . We have reason to believe, that when St. Paul speaks of some at Corinth, that 'they had not repented of the uncleanness which they had committed,' his meaning was, that they had not openly and solemnly humbled themselves in the face of the congregation for their crimes."—*Johnson's Unbloody Sacrifice.*

The same writer continues, " Christians have lost the true notion of perfect repentance for sins after baptism, which the Primitive Church did justly believe to consist in a long course of fasting, praying, confessing openly in the church, deploring and bewailing former sins . . . . This was the ' Repentance to salvation never to be repented of' which the Apostles and Primitive Fathers required of those Christians who had sinned with a high hand.

" It is confessed, that all priests, and none but priests, have power to forgive sins; that private confession to a priest is a very ancient practice in the Church."—*Bishop Montague's Gagger Gagged.*

" Our confession must be *integra* et *perfecta*, not by halves. All our sins must be confessed,—*omnia venialia et omnia mortalia*. God alone blots out sin :—true. But there is another confessor that would not be neglected. He who would be sure of pardon, let him find a priest, and make his humble confession to him. Heaven waits and expects the priest's sentence here, and what he binds or looses, the Lord confirms in Heaven." — *Bishop Sparrow's Sermon on Confession.*

" When you find yourselves charged and oppressed . . . have recourse to your spiritual physician, and freely disclose the nature and malignancy of your disease. Nor come to him only with such mind as you would go to a learned man, as one that can speak comfortable things to you, but as to one that hath authority delegated to him from God himself, to absolve you from your sins."— *Chillingworth.*

" Confession is an excellent institution—a check to vice. It is admirably calculated to win over hearts, which have been ulcerated by hatred, to forgiveness; and to induce those who have been guilty of injustice, to make restitution."— *Voltaire.*

" What restitutions and reparations does not confession produce among the Catholics ! "—*Rousseau.*

Tradition*.

" It is evident, from the Scriptures themselves, that the whole of Christianity was at first delivered to the Bishops

---

* On the truth of the Catholic doctrine, respecting Tradition, the reader will find all that is most cogent and convincing in Dr. Lingard's powerful *Strictures upon Bishop Marsh's Comparative View, &c.* The arguments by which this eminent divine shows that, without the aid of Tradition, the inspiration of the Scriptures themselves cannot be proved, are altogether unanswerable. " How (he asks) can the Scriptures prove their own inspiration? It is on their inspiration that all their doctrinal authority depends. You must show that they are inspired before you can deduce a single point of doctrine from their testimony. If in attempting to demonstrate the inspiration of any book, you pre-suppose its inspiration, you fall into a *petitio principii;* you take for granted what you have undertaken to prove. If you do not pre-suppose its inspiration, then its testimony on that point is of no more authority than the testimony of any profane or ecclesiastical writer . . . . . . Perhaps it may be said that the writers appear, from the tradition of testimony, to have been the apostles of Christ; that they were under the guidance of the Holy Spirit; that they could not teach a false doctrine; and that, of course, their writings must be inspired. But whence is all this information obtained? If from the

succeeding the Apostles, by *oral* tradition, and they were also commanded to keep and deliver it to their successors in *like* manner. Nor is it any where found in Scripture, by St. Paul or any other Apostle, that they would either jointly or separately, write down all they had taught as necessary to salvation, or make such a complete canon of them, that nothing should be necessary to salvation but what should be found in those writings."—*Dr. Brett, Tradition Necessary.*

" Here (2 Thessalon. vi.) we see plain mention of St. Paul's traditions, consequently of Apostolic Traditions, delivered by word of mouth, as well as by writing, and a condemnation of those who do not equally observe both."—*Ibid.*

" Traditions instituted by Christ, in points of faith, have *divine* authority, as the *written* word hath: traditions from the Apostles have equal authority with their writings; and no Protestant in his senses will deny that the Apostles spoke much more than is written."—*Montague's Gagger gagged.*

Dr. Waterland, observing, on the authority of Irenæus, that " Polycarp had converted great numbers to the Faith by the strength of Tradition," adds that it " was a sensible argument, and more affecting at that time than any

---

tradition of testimony, it is then false that the inspiration of the Scripture can be proved from Scripture only: if from the Scripture, then you must prove its inspiration before you can exact the belief of the reader to such assertions. Hence, I conclude, that to determine the Canon or the inspiration of the Scripture from the Scripture alone is impracticable: the knowledge of both must be derived from *Tradition.*

dispute from the bare letter of Scripture could be."—*Imp. of the Doct. of the Trin.*

Prayers for the Dead, and Purgatory.

" Let not the ancient practice of praying and making oblations for the Dead, be any more rejected by Protestants as unlawful. It is a practice received throughout the universal Church of Christ, which did ever believe it both pious and charitable. Many of the Fathers were of opinion that some light sins, not remitted in this life, were forgiven, after death, by the intercession of the Church in her public prayers, and especially those which were offered up in the celebration of the tremendous mysteries; and it is no absurdity to believe so. The practice of praying for the Dead is derived, as Chrysostom asserts, from the Apostles."—*Bishop Forbes, on Purgatory.*

" That Austin concludes, very clearly, that some souls do suffer temporal pains after death cannot be denied."—*Fulke's Confutation of Purgatory.*

After mentioning the different opinions of the Fathers respecting the purgatorial process through which souls are to pass, Leibnitz thus beautifully, and in the true Catholic spirit, concludes:—" Quidquid hujus sit, plerique omnes consenserunt in castigationem sive purgationem post hanc vitam, qualiscunque ea esset, quam ipsæ animæ ab excessu ex corpore, illuminatæ et conspectâ tunc imprimis præteritæ vitæ imperfectione, et peccati fœditate maxima tristitia tactæ sibi accersunt libenter, nollentque aliter ad culmen beatitudinis pervenire."—*Systema Theologicum.*

" There is one proof of the Propitiatory nature of the Eucharist according to the sentiments of the ancient

Church which will be thought but only too great; and that is, the devotions used in the Liturgies and so often spoke of by the Fathers, in behalf of deceased souls. There is, I suppose, no Liturgy without them, and the Fathers frequently speak of them. St. Chrysostom mentions it as an institution of the Apostles. St. Austin asserts that such prayers are beneficial to those who have led lives so moderately good as to deserve them. Cyril of Jerusalem mentions a prayer for those who are gone to sleep before us; and St. Cyprian mentions the denial of those prayers, as a censure passed upon some men by his predecessors. Tertullian spoke of this practice as prevailing in his time, and the Constitutions do require Priests and people to use these sorts of devotion for the souls of those that die in the Faith."—*Johnson's Unbloody Sacrifice.*

"Dr. Whitby," says the same writer, "has fully proved, in his annotations on 2 Tim. iv. 4, that the Primitive Fathers, and even the Apostles, did not believe that the souls of the Faithful are admitted into Heaven before the Day of Judgment. It was, I suppose, from hence concluded that they were, in the interim, in a state of expectance and were capable of an increase of light and refreshment. Since praying for them, while in this state, was nowhere forbidden, they judged it therefore lawful, and if it were lawful, no more need be said,—Nature will do the rest. The only use I make of it is to prove that the ancients believed the Eucharist to be a Propitiatory Sacrifice, and therefore put up these prayers for their deceased friends, in the most solemn part of the Eucharistic Office, after the symbols had received the finishing consecration."

"It must be admitted that there are, in Tertullian's

writings, passages which seem to imply that in the interval between death and the general resurrection, the souls of those who are destined to eternal happiness undergo a purification from the stains which even the best men contract during their lives."—*Bishop Kaye.*

Among Protestant testimonies to this ancient and Christian custom of praying for the Dead, we should not omit the two Epitaphs written for themselves by Bishop Barrow, of St. Asaph, and Mr. Thorndike, Prebendary of Westminster. In the Epitaph of the Bishop are the following words :—" O vos transeuntes in domum Domini, domum orationis, orate pro conservo vestro, ut inveniat misericordiam in die Domini."—" Oh ye, who pass into the House of the Lord, into the House of Prayer, pray for your fellow-servant, that he may find mercy in the day of the Lord." In like manner Thorndike, in his epitaph, entreats that the reader will pray for rest to his soul: " Tu lector requiem ei et beatam in Christo resurrectionem precare."

Invocation of Saints.

" If the Roman Church will declare at once that she has no other confidence in the Saints than in the living, and that in whatsoever terms her prayers to them may be couched, they are to be understood of simple *intercession* alone, that is, ' Holy Mary, pray for me to thy divine Son,'—if, I say, the Catholics will but declare this*, then

---

* Such is, and ever has been, the declaration of Catholics; as will appear from the following exposition of their faith on this point, given in a tract of high authority, entitled *Roman Catholic Principles*, and quoted in that standard work, " the Faith of Catholics."—" Catholics

all danger in such prayers is over."—*Molanus's Answer to Bossuet.*

---

are persuaded that the angels and the saints in heaven replenished with charity, pray for us, the fellow-members of the latter here on earth; that they rejoice in our conversion; that, seeing God, they see and know in him all things suitable to their happy state; and that God may be inclined to hear their requests made in our behalf, and for their sakes may grant us many favours—therefore we believe that it is good and profitable to invoke their intercession. Can this manner of invocation be more injurious to Christ our mediator than it is for one Christian to beg the prayers of another here on earth? However, Catholics are not taught so to rely on the prayers of others as to neglect their own duty to God, in imploring his divine mercy and goodness in mortifying the deeds of the flesh; in despising the world; in loving and serving God and their neighbours; in following the footsteps of Christ our Lord, who is the way, the truth, and the life."

Another point upon which Catholics have, as constantly and as unavailingly, to disclaim the gross notions imputed to them, is their veneration for Holy Pictures and Images—a veneration which they give, "*Not* as believing (says the Council of Trent) that there is in such pictures and images any divinity or virtue for which they should be honoured; or that any thing is to be asked of them, or any trust to be placed in them, as the Gentiles once did on their idols: but because the honour given to pictures is referred to the Prototypes which they represent." In the Catechism of the Roman Catholics, one of the questions asked is, " Whether the Catholics pray to images?"—The answer to which is, " No, they do not;" and this reason is added, " because they neither can see, nor hear, nor help us." So far, indeed, from sanctioning the adoration of Images, the Catholics are accustomed to repeat every week the 97th Psalm, in which are these emphatic words: " Confounded be all they that serve graven images, that boast themselves of idols;" and every Sunday, at Even Song, they repeat Psalm cxv, equally denouncing idols, and containing a sort of imprecation on idolators, that " all

"I do not deny but the Saints are mediators of prayer and intercession for all in general. They interpose with God by their intercessions and mediate by their prayers."—*Bishop Montague, Antidote.*

"Indeed, I grant that Christ is not wronged in his mediation."—*Montague on Invocation of Saints.*

"It is no impiety to say, as Papists say, 'Holy Mary, pray for me!'—Nay, could I come at the Saints, I would, without any question, willingly say, 'Holy Peter, pray for me!' I would run with open arms, fall upon my knees, and desire them to pray for me. I see no absurdity in nature, no repugnancy at all to Scripture, much less impiety, for any man to say 'Holy Angel Guardian, pray for me!'"—*Ib.*

"I confess that Ambrose, Austin, and Jerome, did hold invocation of Saints to be lawful."—*Fulke, Rejoinder to Bristow.*

---

men may become like them (the idols) who make them and put their trust in them."

The great Leibnitz thus philosophically explains and defends the Catholic reverence for images:—" Posito igitur nullam aliam admitti venerationem imaginum quam quæ sit veneratio prototypi coram imagine, non magis in eâ erit idololatria quam in veneratione quæ Deo et Christo exhibetur, sanctissimo ejus nomine pronuntiato. Nam et nomina sunt notæ et quidem imaginibus longè inferiores, rem enim multo minus repræsentant .... coram imagine externa adorare non magis reprehendendum esse quam adorare coram imagine interna quæ in phantasia nostra depicta est: nullus enim alius usus externæ imaginis quam ut interna expressior fiat."—*Systema Theologicum.*

We find Archbishop Wake, as quoted by Middleton, saying, "he did not scruple to declare that, as to the honours due to the genuine relics of the Martyrs or Apostles, no Protestant would ever refuse whatever the Primitive Churches paid to them."

"It is confessed that all the Fathers of both Greek and Latin Churches, Basil, Nazianzen, Ambrose, Jerome, Austin, Chrysostom, Leo, and all after their time, have spoken to the Saints and desired their assistance."— *Thorndyke's Epilogue.*

The Sacrifice in the Eucharist.

" The Sacrifice of the Supper is not only propitiatory and may be offered up for the remission of our daily sins, but impetratory, and may be rightly offered to obtain all blessings; and, though the Scripture does not teach this in express words, yet the Holy Fathers, with unanimous consent, have thus understood the Scriptures, as has been demonstrated by many and must be evident to all."— *Bishop Forbes, de Eucharistia.*

" It seems strange to you ' that a matter of so great importance, as I seem to make this Sacrifice to be, should have so little evidence in God's word and antiquity, and depend merely upon certain conjectures.' As for Scripture, if you mean the *name* of Sacrifice, neither is the *name* Sacrament nor Eucharist (according to our expositions) there to be found,—no more than ὁμοούσιος,—yet may not the *thing* be? But when you speak of so little evidence to be found in *antiquity*, I cannot but think such an affirmation far more strange than you can possibly think my opinion. For, what is there in Christianity for which more antiquity can be brought than for this? . . . . . . Eusebius Altkircherus, a Calvinist, printed at Newstadt, in the Palatinate, in 1584 and 1591, *De Mystico et incruento Ecclesiæ Sacrificio*, in which he says, ' This was always the standing, accordant, and unanimous opinion of all the ancient Fathers of the Church, that the memorial of the passion and death of Christ, in the Holy Supper instituted by him, contained also in itself the commendation of a Sacrifice."—*Mede, Letter to Twisse.*

" I suppose all Protestants will allow that Christ's sacrifice was intended for the expiation of sin; and, if so, they cannot think it strange that it was offered before it was slain, and that by the Priest himself—for it is clear this was the method prescribed by Moses of old. It will presently be shown that the body and blood of Christ were intended as a sacrifice of consecration, as well as expiation, and that therefore the proper time of offering them was before he was actually slain as a sacrifice . . . . And if Christ gave or offered himself in the Eucharist, I presume I need not labour to prove that Priests are to do what he then did. We have his express commands to do or offer this in Remembrance of him, and I have abundantly demonstrated that this was the constant, unanimous judgment of the Primitive Church for the first 400 years after Christ."—*Johnson, Unbloody Sacrifice.*

" There is yet a more evident proof to be found in the Scripture, even in the very words of the Institution, to prove that we are required to *offer* the bread and wine to God, when we celebrate the Holy Eucharist, ' This *do* in remembrance of me.' Dr. Hickes. in his Christian Priesthood, p. 58, &c. proves, by a great many instances, that the word ποιειν, *to do,* also signifies *to offer,* and is very frequently used both by profane authors, and by the Greek translators of the Old Testament in that sense; and so also is the Latin word *facere.* I will transcribe a few of those instances, and those who desire more may consult Dr. Hickes's book.

" Herodotus, lib. 1, cap. cxxxii, says, ' Without one of

the Magi, it is not lawful for them, ποιειν, to offer a sacrifice.' And in the Septuagint translation of the Old Testament, which all the learned know is followed by the writers of the New Testament, even where they cite the words and speeches of our Saviour, it is so used; as Exod. xxix. 36, ' Thou shalt offer, ποιησεις, a bullock ;' verse 38, ' This is that which, ποιησεις, thou shalt offer upon the altar ;' verse 39, ' The one lamb, ποιησεις, thou shalt offer in the morning, and the other lamb, ποιησεις, thou shalt offer in the evening.' So likewise Exod. x. 25. In all which places the word, which is translated *offer*, and which in this last text is translated *sacrifice*, and which in these and many other places will bear *no other* sense, is the very word which in the institution of the Eucharist is translated *Do*. And even our English translators have sometimes used the word *Do* in this sacrificial sense; as particularly Lev. iv. 20. Here our English translation is, ' And he shall *do* with the bullock, as he *did* with the bullock for a sin offering, so shall he *do* with this.' Here, indeed, they have put in the word *with*, without any authority. The Greek is, ' he shall *do* the bullock, as he *did* the bullock, so shall he *do* this ;' where *do* plainly signifies *offer*. . . . . . . That the words of the institution, τουτο ποιειτε, *do this*, are to be understood in this sacrificial sense, is manifest from the command concerning the cup, which is, ' This *do* ye, as oft as you drink it, in remembrance of me.' For except we understand the words in such a sense, they will be a plain tautology. But translate it, as I have showed the words will very probably bear, ' *Offer this :* make an oblation or libation of this, *as oft as ye drink it in remembrance of me*,' and the sense is very good. A Priest therefore is necessary and essential to the due administration of the sacrament."—*Dr. Brett, True Scrip. Account of the Eucharist.*

For the best *Catholic* arguments on all the above points, I beg to refer to the Earl of Shrewsbury's comprehensive and able *Reasons for not taking the Test, &c.*, and Dr. Baines's lively and acute Answers to Archdeacon Daubeny, &c.

Page 86.

" *The Eucharist prefigured in the offerings of the Old Law.*"

Clement of Alexandria, among the rest, expressly says, that Melchisedeck distributed bread and wine, as consecrated food, for a *type* of the Eucharist:—την ηγιασμενην διδους τροφην εις τυπον ευχαριστιας.—*Stromat. Lib. 4.*

Page 89.

" *If it had so great power in the type, &c.*"

In the same sense, Eusebius says, " We with good reason, daily celebrating the memorial of Christ's body and blood, and being dignified with a better victim and Hierurgy than the old people, do not think it safe to fall back to the former weak elements that contain *symbols and images, not the Verity.*"—ουκ ετι εσιον ηγουμεθα καταπιπτειν επι τα πρωτα και ασθενη στοιχεια συμβολα και εικονα, αλλ' ουκ αυτην αληθειαν περιεχοντα.—*Demoustrat. Evangel.*

Page 102.

To Schelstrate, who held that the Discipline of the Secret was in full force of operation, during the second century, this instance of boldness, on the part of St. Justin, in promulgating the doctrine of Transubstantiation to the Gentiles, appears naturally a disconcerting and puzzling fact. " Cum enim Romanum Senatum Gentilem tunc fuisse, Antoninum quoque cum ejus filiis Paganos extitisse, certum sit, ostendi debet quomodo, salvâ disciplinâ Arcani tam clarè de Baptismi ritibus et Eucharistiæ Sacramentis tractare potuerit Justinus." His solution of the difficulty is, that Justin was led to so daring a step by the necessity of vindicating the Christians against the calumnies of which they were then the object.

Page 117.

Among the clearest and strongest arguments that have been advanced as well for the application of John vi. to the Eucharist as for the connexion of the Eucharist itself with the Incarnation, may be accounted those brought forward by the famous Bretschneider in his Treatise on the Gospel and Epistles of St. John; nor is the opinion of this writer the less worthy of attention from his being himself wholly uninterested in the decision of the question, (at least, as it stands between Protestants and Catholics,) the object of his book being no less than to prove that this Gospel was not written by St. John at all, but by some Gnostic impostor of a later period.

I shall here subjoin, for the learned reader, a passage from this Treatise, in which, comparing the account given of the Docetæ by Ignatius, and the repugnance felt by these heretics to the doctrine of a Real Presence, with the announcements made by Jesus in the sixth Chapter of St. John, Bretschneider shows that our Saviour's language was directed against their heresy, and had no other object than to establish, in opposition to their views, the reality and verity of his own flesh in the Sacrament:—

" Non vero omnibus eandem fuisse sententiam, et Docetas nominatim negasse in eucharistia adesse Jesu carnem s. corpus, ex Ignatii epistolis videmus, quae vel maxime non sint genuinae, tamen haud dubie seculo secundo debentur. Hic vero, et quidem epist. ad Smyrnaeos c 6. p. 37. ed. Cleric., legitur locus, mirum in modum cum nostro congruens. Ignatius enim de Docetis, εὐχαριστίας, inquit, καὶ προσευχης (i. e. precum in eucharistia faciendarum, puto της ἐπικλησεως του πνευματος ἁγιου) ἀπεχονται δια το μη ὁμολογειν την εὐχαριστιαν σαρκα εἰναι του σωτηρος ἡμων Ἰησου Χριστου, την ὑπερ ἁμαρτιων ἡμων παθουσαν, ἡν τη χρηστοτητι ὁ πατηρ ἡγειρεν· οἱ οὖν ἀντι λεγοντες τῃ δωρεᾳ του Θεου, συζητουντες ἀποθνησκουσι· συνεφερεν δε αὐτοις ἀγαπᾳν (i. e. agapen celebrare) ἱνα και ἀναστωσουσιν.—

" Vide vero, quam apta sint ea, quae Jesu in nostro loco tribuuntur, ad refellendos ejusmodi eucharistiae contemtores!

" 1. *Negant:* την εὐχαριστιαν σαρκα εἰναι του Ἰησου, την ὑπερ ἁμαρτιων ἡμων παθουσαν.

" 1. Affirmavit Jesus v. 51: ὁ ἀρτος ὁν ἐγω δωσω ἡ σαρξ μου ἐστιν, ἡν ἐγω δωσω ὑπερ της του κοσμου ζωης. v 55: ἡ σαρξ μου ἀληθως ἐστι βρωσις, και το αἱμα μου ἀληθως ἐστι ποσις.

"2. Appellatur σαρξ Christi δωρεα του Θεου.

"3. Dicuntur adversarii eucharistiae et corporis domini συζητουντες αποθνησκειν, sine spe immortalitatis esse, cum contra si eucharistia uterentur efficeretur ἱνα και αναστωσιν, ut etiam ipsi, ut reliqui fideles, resurgerent ad vitam.

"2. Dicitur σαρξ v. 51. 58. αρτος, ὁ εκ του ουρανου καταβας.

"3. Docet Jesus: majorem judaeorum panem coelestem Mosis quidem comedisse, sed tamen mortuos esse, v. 49. 58.—negat, v. 53: ἐαν μη φαγητε την σαρκα του υιου του ανθρωπου, και πιητε αυτου το αἱμα, ουκ ἐχετε ζωην ἐν ἑαυτοις—affirmat, contra: ὁ τρωγων μου την σαρκα, και πινων μου το αἱμα, ἐχει ζωην αἰωνιον. και ἐγω αναστησω αυτον τη ἐσχατη ἡμερα. Idem promiv. 50. 51. 57."

Page 118.

Remarking on the lame and impotent manner, in which Dr. Whitby endeavours to explain away the import of 1 Cor. x. 16, 17, Johnson says, " The most that the learned Dr. Whitby can make out of this is,—' The Bread broken and shared out may be said to be the Communion or Communication of the Body of Christ as being the communication of that Bread which represented his broken body; and the Cup they severally drink of may be styled the Communication of the Blood of Christ, as being the communication of that wine that represented his bloodshed ' *It may be said, it may be styled*, says the Doctor,—by which it is intimated that, if it be so said or styled, it is in a very remote and improper sense, only so as to bring our Saviour and the Apostle off from being guilty of an absurdity."

In reference to Whitby's attempt to class the text of "This bread is my body" with "the Three Branches are three days"—"the seven good kine are seven years" (Gen. xli. 26), "The four great beasts are four kings" (Dan. vii. 17), "Thou art that head of gold" (Dan. ii. 38), Johnson remarks, "So that it should seem the bread of the Eucharist is, in the Doctor's judgment, no otherwise the body of Christ than the visionary Head of Gold was Nebuchadnezzar."! He then adds, "Our Saviour having positively affirmed 'It is my body,' Dr. Whitby, in good manners, thinks himself obliged not to contradict Christ Jesus, and therefore confesses it *may be so said, it may be so styled*, just as the Three Branches are said to be Three Days. But Irenæus, Justin Martyr, and Ignatius did not thus expound away the life and efficacy of the Sacrament into mere cold and empty types."

Page 119.

The learned writer just referred to cites the following remarkable passage from St. Augustine, confirmatory alike of the two Catholic points of belief, the high authority of Tradition, and the vital nature of the Eucharist, as asserted in John vi.—'The Punick Christians do rightly call Baptism nothing but Salvation, and the Sacrifice of the Body of Christ nothing but Life.—And whence have they this but from an ancient and, I think, apostolical Tradition, by which they hold it to be a principle innate in the Church of Christ that the kingdom of Heaven (or Salvation) cannot be had without Baptism. And what do they hold who call the Sacrament of the Lord's Table,

Life, but that which was said, ' I am the Bread of Life, and except ye eat of the flesh of the Son of Man and drink his blood, ye have no life in you.' " " This (remarks Johnson) is a most ample testimony that the African Churches did believe John vi. to be meant of the Sacrament; and it seems this way of speaking was of so long standing that St. Austin thought it an Apostolic Tradition, an innate principle of Christianity—' quâ Ecclesiæ Christi institutum tenent.'"

Page 120.

" In speaking of those heretics who abstained from the Eucharist, Ignatius pronounces sentence upon them in these words, ' It were better for them to receive it (the Eucharist), that, through it, they might one day rise again.' Now, that the Eucharist is the means of a happy resurrection cannot be allowed to be the doctrine of Scripture, except John vi. be meant of the Eucharist, and therefore this Holy Martyr, when he does once and again assert that this is a privilege conferred on us by the Eucharist must, of consequence, be of this sentiment that our Saviour there spoke of his sacramental body and blood."

" Moreover, I insist that there were several doctrines which prevailed in the first ages of Christianity that could not be grounded on any other authority of Scripture than this of John vi., as understood of the Eucharist, viz.— that by abstaining from the Holy Eucharist Christians do incur the penalty of eternal damnation,—that the Holy Spirit is particularly present in the Eucharist,—that the Eucharist conveys to all worthy receivers a principle of happy immortality."—*Johnson.*

"The ancients knew," adds the same writer, "that our Saviour there spoke of the Eucharist, and they did by no means believe that Christ in the Holy Sacrament feeds the souls of men with mere dry metaphors or catachreses. Though they did not understand Christ in a literal sense, as the Capernaites did, yet neither, on the other hand, did they suppose that it was the intention of Christ to puzzle his auditors, and even stagger his own disciples, with strained enigmatical sayings,—for they believed he spoke of a real mystery; and that he was now opening his intention of establishing the most divine Sacrament of his Flesh and Blood, and to raise in them just thoughts and apprehensions of that heavenly Mystery, he speaks of it in the most elevated words."

Page 121.

CONNEXION BETWEEN THE EUCHARIST AND THE MYSTERY OF THE INCARNATION.

"The difficulties," says the Rev. Mr. Rutter, "which Protestants allege against Transubstantiation are not greater than those which the Socinians may and do urge against the Incarnation: as will appear from the following parallel:—

Protestants reject Transubstantiation,	The Socinians may equally reject the Incarnation,
1. Because the senses judge the host to be mere bread.	1. Because the senses judge Christ to be a mere man.
2. Because one body will be in two or more places.	2. Because one person will be in two natures.

3. Because the same body will move and not move, be visible and not visible, mortal and immortal, passible and impassible.

3. Because the same person will be both God and man, visible and not visible, mortal and immortal, passible and impassible, &c.

4. Because Christ would be in the form of a wafer.

4. Because an immense God would be in the form of a simple man.

5. Because Christ's body would be in a form opposite to human nature.

5. Because God would be in a form opposite to the divine nature.

6. Because Christ's body would be eaten by sinners.

6. Because God would be crucified by sinners.

7. How can Christ's body be confined in the tabernacle, and be also in heaven?

7. How can Christ be confined in the womb of a virgin, and be also in heaven?

8. Because it appears absurd to adore Christ in the sacrament.

8. Because it appears absurd to adore him who was born of a woman, and afterwards crucified by man.

Page 128.

" St. Justin, in affirming that Christians were, in his time, instructed that the Bread and Wine *were* the Flesh and Blood, and that they were *made* so by Prayer, must intend something more than naked types; for there is no occasion for Prayer, or for the Divine Concurrence, *toties quoties*, to render any thing a resemblance of another; and I dare say that the Arminians and Socinians will bear witness that nothing but breaking the bread and pouring out the wine is necessary to make the elements the Body and Blood in their sense, who believe them to be nothing more than mere memorandums."—*Johnson.*

Page 130.

In his Homily on the 10th chapter of the first Epistle to the Corinthians, v. 16, 17, St. Chrysostom says, " The Apostle speaks so as to make us *believe* and *tremble*, for he asserts, that what is in the cup is that which flowed out of Christ's side, and of this we partake." In referring to this passage, Johnson pertinently asks, " What is there in *a Type* to make a man *tremble?*"

Page 147.

A curious testimony to the strictness with which, on the subject of the Eucharist, the Discipline of the Secret continued to be observed even in the Fourth Century is to be found in the arguments brought forward by Deylingius against Peiresc, on the subject of a coin of Constantine the Great, discovered by the latter, upon which he had persuaded himself he could trace the figure of an altar, bearing on it the Eucharistic wafer, or Host. Deylingius, a fierce opponent of the Sacrifice of the Mass, and therefore interested in getting rid of all proofs of its antiquity, contended, and I believe with truth (as far as the coin was concerned) that the round figure which Peiresc took for the Host was but the common emblem of the " globus mundi,"—that, at the time when the coin was struck, Constantine had not yet been baptized, and could therefore know nothing of the Eucharist; and that, even *had* he known of it, the rules of the Discipline of the

Secret would have prevented his revealing to the Pagans any thing connected with such a mystery.

Page 172.

"*Testimonies of the Fathers respecting the Eucharist.*"

To these extracts, on the subject of the Eucharist, I shall venture to add a few more which seem to have escaped the notice of my friend, and for which I am indebted to the invaluable work of the Rev. Mr. Berington, " The Faith of Catholics."

Origen.—" In former times, Baptism was obscurely represented in the cloud and in the sea, but now regeneration is in kind, in water and in the Holy Ghost. Then, obscurely, manna was the food; but now, in kind, the *flesh of the Word of God is the true food;* even, as he said, ' My flesh is meat indeed, and my blood is drink indeed.' "—*Hom. 7, in Num.*

St. Ambrose.—" If *Heretics deny that adoration should be paid to the mysteries* of the Incarnation of Jesus Christ, they may read in the Scripture, that the Apostles also adored him, after he had risen again in a glorified body." He then speaks of " *the very flesh of Jesus Christ, which, to this day, we adore in our sacred mysteries.*" (Quam hodie quoque in mysteriis adoramus.)

St. Gaudentius.—" Believe what is announced to thee; because what thou receivest is the body of that celestial bread, and the blood of that sacred vine; for when he delivered consecrated bread and wine to his disciples, thus he said, ' This is my body, this is my blood.' *Let us believe him, whose faith we profess; for truth cannot lie.*"—*Tract. II. de Pasch.*

St. Gregory of Nyssa.—" It is by virtue of the benediction that the nature of the visible species is changed into his body. The bread, also, is at first common bread, but when it has been sanctified it is called, and is made the body of Christ. Τη της ευλογιας δυναμει προς εκεινο μεταστοιχειωσας των φαινομενων την φυσιν."—*Orat. in Bapt. Christi.*

Before those heretical notions which prevailed, respecting the Trinity and the Real Presence, had rendered it necessary, in speaking of these mysteries, to employ a word denoting actual *substance*, the Fathers of the Church employed a variety of terms to describe the change which takes place in the Eucharist. Μετοστοιχιωσις is, we see, the phrase used in the passage just cited, by Gregory of Nyssa. In Theophylact we find Μεταποιησις employed for the same purpose, and the different words, Μεταβολη, Μετασχηματισμος, Μεταρρυθμισις, Μετασκευασμος, have each been used, by some one or other of the Fathers, to express the miraculous change. When the Phantastic heretics, however, had begun to spiritualize away the reality of the Presence, and the opposers of the Trinity to resolve into mere concord and consent the mysterious Oneness of the Father and Son, it became necessary for the orthodox to assert the *substantiality* in both mysteries; and hence the introduction of those two words, equally unauthorized by Scripture—Consubstantial and Transubstantiation.

Page 175.

In the Liturgy used by St. Cyril of Jerusalem we find the sense both of himself and his Church expressed—
Παρακαλουμεν τον φιλανθρωπον Θεον το αγιον πνευμα εξαποςτειλαι

επι τα προκειμενα ινα ποιηση τον μεν αρτον σωμα Χριστου τον δε οινον αιμα Χριστου· παντως γαρ 'ου αν εφαψαιτο το άγιον πνευμα τουτο ηγιασται και μεταβεβληται. " We beseech of God, the lover of souls, to send down his Holy Spirit upon these gifts laid in open view, that he may make the bread the body of Christ and the wine the blood of Christ. For, to whatever the Holy Ghost gives a contact, that thing is *consecrated and changed.*"

Page 185.

" *The special selection by the Christians of those Days for Festivals,*" &c.

" On voit par le Calendrier de Bucherus et par d'autres que les Romains avoient le 25 Decembre une fête marquée Dies Invicti, en l'honneur du retour du Soliel. Elle se faisait avec de grandes réjouissances. Ce fut apparemment pour s'opposer à la licence de cette Fête que l'Eglise Romaine plaça en ce même jour celle de la naissance de Jesus Christ. De même qu'on institua la procession du jour de S. Marc, pour l'opposer à celle que faisoient les Païens ce même jour 25 Avril, en l'honneur du Dieu Rubigo, et les luminaires de la fête de la Purification tout de même." —*Longuerue.*

On comparing my friend's account of the numerous instances in which the early Christians borrowed from Paganism, with the famous Letter of Middleton, in which the same task is, with a very different object, undertaken, the reader will perceive how meagre and limited were Middleton's inquiries on the subject.

Page 206.

The following is the grave and matter of fact language in which Luther described his theological controversy with the Devil:—" Contigit me semel sub mediam noctem subitò expergefieri. Ibi Satan mecum cœpit ejusmodi disputationem. Audé inquit, Luthere, doctor perdocte. Noctè etiam te quindecim annis celebrasse massas privatùs penè quotidiè? Quod si tales massæ privatæ horrenda esset idololatria? Cui respondi, sum unctus sacerdos . . . hæc omnia feci ex mandato et obedientia majorum: hæc nosti. Hoc inquit, totum est verum; sed Turcæ et Gentilis etiam faciunt omnia in suis templis ex obedientiâ. In his angustiis, in hoc agone contra Diabolum volebam retundere hostem armis quibus assuetus sum sub papatu, &c. Verum Satan è contra, fortius et vehementius instans, age, inquit, prome ubi scriptum est quod homo impius possit consecrare, &c., &c. Hæc fere erat disputationis summa."—*De Unct. et Mis. Privat.*

Chillingworth supposes that the intention of Satan in arguing against the Mass was to induce his antagonist to persevere in saying it. (*Relig. of Prot.*)

Page 218.

" My flesh which I will give for the Life of the world."

" Nor are we to wonder if Christ made something else besides Faith and obedience to the moral laws necessary to eternal salvation. Man, even in Paradise, had a positive Law given him, over and above the Laws of Nature and of Reason, namely, that he should not eat of the fruit of the Tree of Good and Evil. If he had even obeyed in this, he could not have attained eternal happiness without eating the Tree of Life,—to show that eternal Life and perfect obedience are two things that have no necessary dependence on each other. For the same reason he hath required Christians not only to believe and obey in other respects, but, in order to secure ourselves a happy resurrection, he directs us to feed on the Bread of Life, the Holy Eucharist. For, by making this a necessary condition, without which we cannot attain immortal happiness, he gives us a demonstration that Eternal Life is the gift of God, and not the wages of our righteousness and obedience. When therefore our Saviour says, ' He that believeth in me hath eternal life,' the meaning is, not that Faith alone is sufficient to salvation, but that a true believer, by being a member of Christ's Church and enjoying the Eucharist, has the means of eternal life provided for him by Christ Jesus, as Adam, by living in Paradise, and having the Fruit of the Tree of Life within his reach, might be said to have eternal life; and it is very observable how unanimous the ancient writers of the Church are, not only in asserting that this Sacrament is necessary to Salvation, but that it is the means by which our bodies have a principle of a happy resurrection conveyed to them."—*Johnson.*

Page 225. *Note.*

" But the Sacrament was an institution perfectly new and unheard of before, when our Saviour first administered it, in the opinion of those who deny John vi. to relate to this matter. It therefore must be supposed that our Saviour did extempore institute and oblige his Apostles to receive the Sacrament without giving them any previous notice or information whereby they might be prepared for it,—unless it be acknowledged that here, in this context, he did give them this notice ; for we have not the least intimation of his doing so in any other place of the Histories of the Evangelists. And, therefore, to acquit our Saviour of any such imputation, it ought in reason to be acknowledged that he did it here; and that St. John, observing that the other Evangelists had omitted this discourse, thought it necessary to be inserted in his Gospel; whereas, the history of the Institution being related by the other three, there was no occasion for him to repeat it."—*Ib.*

Page 249.

" *To show how opposite were the characters of the Jewish and the Christian God.*"

" The difference between the style of the Old and New Testament is so very remarkable, that one of the greatest sects in the primitive times did, upon this very ground, found their heresy of Two Gods; the one evil, fierce, and cruel, whom they called the God of the Old Testament; the other good, kind, and merciful, whom they called the God of the New Testament. So great a difference is there between the representations which are made of God, in the Books of the Jewish and Christian religions, as to give at least some colour and pretence for an Imagination of two Gods."—*Tillotson.*

Page 273.

In giving an account of the Carpocratians, another branch of these Gnostics, the author of L'Histoire du Gnosticisme, says:—" C'est la Gnosis, c'est la science des Carpocratiens qui donne cette science. Ce n'est pourtant ni une science nouvelle ni une science exclusive; elle a été donnée à tous les peuples, ou plutôt les grands hommes de tous les peuples ont pu s'élever jusqu'à elle—

Payens ou Juifs, Pythagore, Platon, Aristote, Moise et Jesus Christ ont possédé cette gnosis, la Vérité. Cette Gnosis affranchit des lois du monde (Η αληθεια ελευθερωσει ὑμας)—elle fait plus ; elle affranchit de tout ce que le vulgaire appelle Religion." In a note, the author adds :—
" Voilà une école *méprisable* qui proclame il y a seize siècles l'Universalisme le plus philosophique et le plus religieux que connaisse notre tems."

Page 275.

" *The Gnostics forerunners of the Anabaptists,*" &c.

Of the Carpocratians, the historian of Gnosticism says, " Tout ce que les docteurs orthodoxes appeloient les *bonnes œuvres* ils le traitoient de choses extérieures, indifférentes . . . . C'est par *la foi* et sans les œuvres que les orthodoxes se recommendaient à côté d'elles." The similarity between these fanatics and the ravers of the Reformation did not escape the observation of this writer. " Rien," he says, " ne nous parait plus propre à faire juger les Carpocratiens de la Cyrenaïque que les anabaptistes de Munster."

END OF VOL. I.